...n of

13

FORTIES FASHION
AND THE NEW LOOK

COLIN McDOWELL

FORTIES FASHION

AND

THE NEW LOOK

BLOOMSBURY

Acknowledgements

I have been given considerable help from the library staffs of National Magazine Company and the London College of Fashion, and from the staff of the Imperial War Museum. I spoke to many women who had memories of the war, specifically in Gloucestershire, the West Midlands, the North East, South Wales and London. Their reminiscences were invaluable but this is not a book of oral history. For that, I recommend *We Wore What We'd Got*, a selection of comments by Warwickshire women compiled by Maggie Wood for Warwickshire County Council. For those wishing to learn more about taste and social attitudes, as well as fashion, during the war there are no better sources than women's magazines. *Vogue* and *Harper's Bazaar*, *Good Housekeeping* and *Woman's Journal* are invaluable, but so are the less prestigious, more basic magazines, most of which are long defunct, but still to be found in specialist libraries.

Special thanks to Catherine Baird, librarian of the London College of Fashion, for her individual help in this project, and to Jenny de Gex for her picture research.

First published in Great Britain 1997
Bloomsbury Publishing Plc, 38 Soho Square, London W1V 6HB

A CIP catalogue record for this book is available from the British Library

ISBN 0 7475 3032 7

10 9 8 7 6 5 4 3 2

Designed by Bradbury and Williams
Designer: Bob Burroughs

Printed in Great Britain by Butler & Tanner Ltd, Frome

Title-page: 'Offenbach' by Christian Dior, an evening gown in the grand manner.

Contents

FOREWORD

BY DARCEY BUSSELL

It is hard for me to picture my late grandmother looking anything but glamorous. She seemed always to be beautifully dressed in the most elegant tailored suits, with knee-length pencil skirts and fitted jackets, and she never wore flat shoes (I am told that she owned about a hundred and twenty pairs of high heels – what luxury!). She also had quite the most enormous collection of silk scarves and shawls I've ever seen, all simply exquisite and many worn by my mother and me now. Her hair was red – though it turned a lovely shade of pink as she got older – and always impeccably curled; and even in her later years she had fantastic legs. (Apparently, her legs were always one of her most attractive features: my grandfather, at one time a Hollywood photographer, had dated Betty Grable – known, of course, for her wonderful legs – and when he and my grandmother were first dating he wrote her a note saying that Betty's legs were 'not a patch' on hers!) As a child, it seemed to me that her wardrobe held no end of exciting dressing-up potential – shoes to clop around in, scarves, feather boas, bags and wide-brimmed hats – a perfect collection for any young girl with modish aspirations!

Perhaps it's because of these memories of my grandmother's style that I so love the fashion of the Forties. She certainly epitomised the glamour of the era, and stimulated my interest in the classic sophistication one associates with the models and stars of the time. Since I was quite young I have found the fashion of the Forties and the New Look enormously attractive. The elegance and composure of the models in those timeless black and white photographs of the period is incredible – they always looked so relaxed and comfortable while in such classic and stylised poses (I have a number of good-luck cards all over my dressing-room, sent before performances, featuring just those kinds of images).

Many of the principal ballerinas of the Forties became icons of glamour, in the same way that film stars were, and were often asked to wear the top designers' clothes to parties and on tour. During the war, companies toured everywhere by train; not the most luxurious mode of transport but, I have been told, the girls would get off still looking as pristine as they did when they'd boarded – because of their smart suits, matching gloves and bags (and, maybe, because of those fabulous big trunks in which they carried their clothes!).

Margot Fonteyn was, of course, especially chic, and one of my idols as a dancer, so I was delighted to learn that as part of their exhibition the Imperial War Museum has one of Dior's first New Look coats, which had belonged to her and had no doubt been the source of much admiration at the time. (In addition they have a pair of the beautiful slippers worn by Moira Shearer in *The Red Shoes*, a film which as a young dancer I watched in awe.) Now, of course, it is not quite as important for dancers to look so well-presented all the time; despite generous offers from many designers willing to lend their clothes to me for public appearances I'm afraid I worry about damaging them on tour! It is, nevertheless, wonderful to feel chic on important occasions, and I imagine it must have been great to feel so smart and look so good all the time!

The less glamorous side of Forties fashion is of no less interest to me. It has been fascinating to look at examples of clothes made during such difficult times, both in terms of finance and morale. What strikes me is that so many outfits worn by working women perfectly emulated the style of the designers; though money was short, looking smart was important and the look of the era was such that with simple, cleanly cut clothes women could feel stylish for very little cost.

Some of the home-made garments I have seen are quite lovely, their charm lying not only in their distinctly personal feel, but also in the sense of initiative so evident in them – and so pertinent to the circumstances under which they were made. A nice example of Make Do and Mend is a blouse made from a silk map of the type sold in the UK – women were advised that if they first washed the starch out of the material it was ideal for making clothes. The stories behind some of the items appeal to me too: the wife of a serviceman in Austria who turned a captured German flag into a beautiful dressing-gown, which she wore during the couple's first holiday together after the war; and the amateur tap dancers who made dresses for their performances out of blackout material.

It has been a delight to be involved with this book and with the Imperial War Museum's exhibition. It has rekindled my long-time love for the fashion of the Forties, the romance, sophistication and understated glamour of the era, and, most of all, has brought back many fond memories of my grandmother in all her splendour.

INTRODUCTION

BY HARDY AMIES

In the Thirties in the couture houses – and by couture I mean the genuine bespoke stuff, not just expensive – in Paris and London, there was a marked theme. This was an interest in the bosom. These darling little objects had been flattered in the new, short-skirted, bob-haired look of the Twenties. To everyone' s surprise, Schiaparelli made the clothes for a Mae West film. Bosoms were to the fore. In my Spring Collection in 1938 I sent the girls out in old-fashioned stays and black bloomers. This little bud remained closed until the full bloom of the New Look in 1947.

Throughout the Thirties buyers came regularly to couture houses to buy models to take away to copy. Paris got higher prices for a model than they did from a private customer. London suits (the term coat and skirt lived on only in upper circles) were considered better than those of Paris. Buyers attached to the large stores in New York, San Francisco and Toronto came faithfully each season. The Board of Trade became interested in the growing volume of exports from the couture houses. In 1942 these houses, at that time numbering ten, united themselves, at the Board' s request, into the Incorporated Society of London Fashion Designers. I was admitted as a private member (I had no fashion house, having left Lachasse in 1939 to join the army). The members of INCSOC, as it was called, took a joint collection to New York and Paris.

INCSOC was founded by Harry Yoxall, managing editor of London *Vogue*. The editress was Audrey Withers. It was customary to have a grand English lady as chairman of INCSOC. Pam Berry, Anne Rothermere and Jane Clark spring to mind – they were wonderful hostesses when required to be.

Since the days of Mrs Edna Chase, the doyenne of all fashion editors in New York, the English style had been held in high regard. English clothes reflected that style. London clothes had to be at home in the country and, to balance this, country clothes had to look happy in London.

All this flourished during the 'Phoney War', but houses still produced collections even after the bombs started to drop.

I had become an officer in the newly formed Intelligence Corps and was posted to the Canadian Corps, where there were few staff officers. My boss, John Tweedsmuir, was surprised to hear that the Board of Trade had applied for me to have six weeks' leave to help with a collection to go to South Africa. Why South Africa was chosen I shall never know, but I enjoyed getting away from headquarters.

When the Canadians got their own Intelligence officers, I was moved to the Belgian Section of the famous Special Operations Executive (SOE). We had to train agents in the art of sabotage and parachute them into Belgium, behind the German

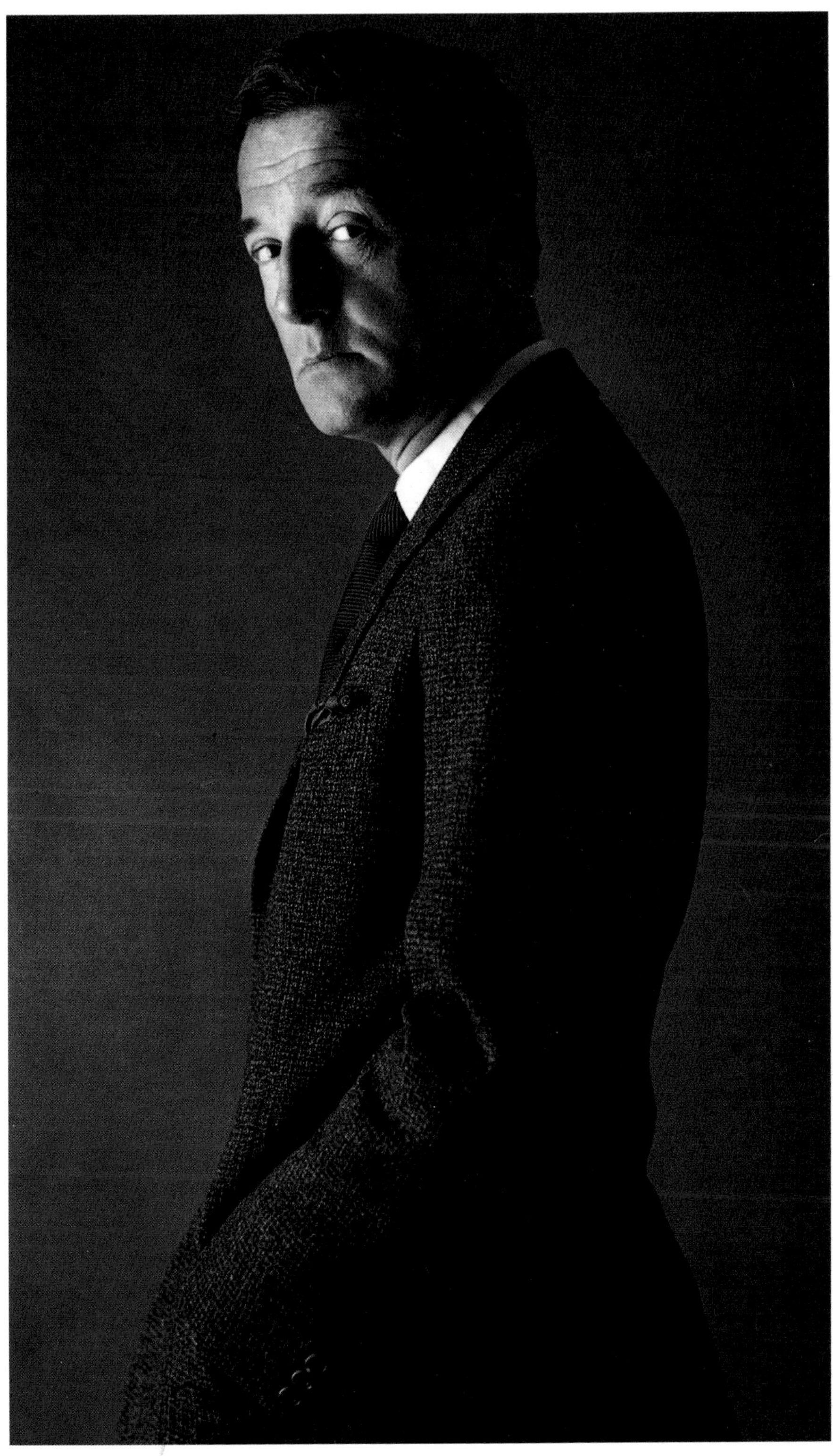

Sir Hardy Amies served with the Intelligence Corps during the war, reaching the rank of Lt Colonel, but he was still allowed time to continue designing for the 'export drive'.

lines. It was not joyful work. One suspected that the Belgian Resistance movements were seriously penetrated by the Germans and that our men were sometimes dropped not into Belgian but into German hands.

Very early in the war moves were made to stop women wearing jewellery and other potentially dangerous fashion items near machinery.

Patience and valour were eventually rewarded with the news that the Germans had evacuated Brussels. The next day my staff and I moved into a flat there, in the rue Belliard. I had been effectively head of the office for some time, but not formally installed. It was thought that our opposite numbers in the Belgian army would not be flattered that their English counterpart was a dressmaker. I was given the rank of lieutenant colonel to sustain dignity.

After the austerity of wartime London it was pleasant to see shops full of luxury. The women were splendidly dressed, often in clothes from Paris. The bicycle controlled day clothes. Skirts were short and pleated; suit coats had military shoulders.

these are unfashionable...
near running machinery

With the Germans gone from Brussels I felt the war was over. I began to plan my future. I would not go back to Lachasse. I had an offer from Worth of London. No, sir, I wanted my own business. When the Board of Trade heard of this they applied to the army for my early release.

The London offices of SOE were in Baker Street. There I led the life of any employee of an office organisation. I became friendly with the famous international couturier, Edward Molyneux. He had fled to London when the Germans invaded Paris. It was quite natural that he should become the first Chairman of INCSOC.

Molyneux was Irish, born in 1894; he worked in London with the first 'grande dame' dressmaker, Lucile, and after a distinguished war career (I mean, of course, the 1914-18 war) he opened his shop in Paris in 1919. In 1930 he opened in London under the direction of his sister Kathleen. I speak of shops because I cannot bear the word 'salon' — but of course dress houses were like grand private houses. At Molyneux's at 48 Grosvenor Street you were greeted by a butler.

Molyneux settled into a suite at Claridges, the walls hung with pictures from his collection. He himself was a painter of no inconsiderable talent. I was given the freedom of his house and often attended his fittings. He was carrying on supplying models to his favourite stores in the USA. Princess Marina of Kent was his star customer.

'I remove everything that is not necessary,' he said. 'Plainness is all.' But he paid great attention to cut, finish and, above all, proportion. Molyneux loved English tweeds. His evening dresses were astonishingly simple. 'They've all got jewellery,' he said. He never seemed interested in jewellery. When Utility regulations were introduced, we both laughed. 'We have been making utility clothes for years,' we said.

After the war Molyneux went back to Paris to his dress house, which he closed in 1950. It is amazing to me that no book has appeared in English on this great man. He was, without question, the most talented designer of clothes that Britain has ever produced. He was also, of course, a couturier of the highest order. He had a great influence on me. He showed me how the sobriety of English style could become international chic.

I am tremendously pleased to have been asked to write this introduction. The task has brought back many memories. Above all it has reminded me how lucky I have been. I have spoken of my indebtedness to *Vogue*, and of Audrey Withers. This piece was published by *Vogue* in January 1947.

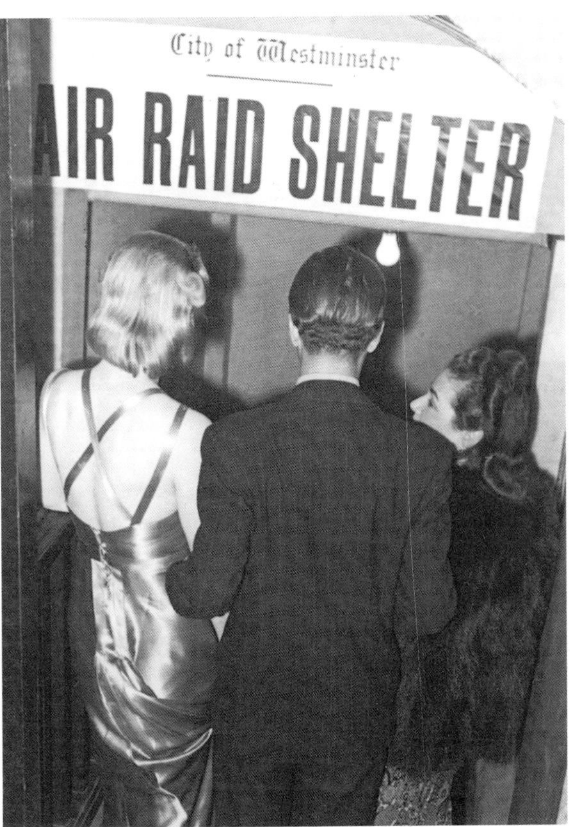

During the 'phoney war' London's nightclubs remained open, but many had air raid shelters like this one at the Paradise Club in the West End.

'Hardy Amies is, despite a French-German education, very much the "type anglais". Before he became liaison officer to the British and Belgian Armies in Brussels he designed at Lachasse, and during the war he continued designing for export at Worth. Now he has taken Sheridan's old house at 14 Savile Row, and it hums with painters, workmen and alterations. His soft woollen dresses, suits and coats are a perfect foil for Englishwomen, but he is really in love with the dinner dresses and *robes d'intérieur* which he does so well. Collections, he says, grow out of each other, because fashion is an evolvement, but even so a fashion may wait as long as a year for acceptance. In the army he saw clothes from a new viewpoint – in action and unstudied: found it interesting and salutary. Ideas often take shape during country weekends, or while studying his fine collection of old fashion books.'

I wish Colin McDowell all success with his book, and my blessings to the organiser of the exhibition it accompanies.

Hardy Amies
September 1996

CHAPTER 1

Last Trumpets, First Bugles

Left: Jean Harlow, sophisticated screen siren. Above: Hat and gloves – hallmark of the lady.

The Thirties! Even more evocative than the Twenties, they were a decade of glamour and sophistication made all the more poignant in retrospect by the Forties and the privations and hardships they brought. They were also a decade of contrasts so extreme that pinpointing their character, especially in fashion, is not easy.

Were the Thirties the masculine chic of Wallis Simpson or the soft femininity of Queen Elizabeth? The slinky evening dresses of Jean Harlow or the well-tailored pants of Katharine Hepburn? The picture hats and flowing chiffons of Ascot or the cotton dirndls and shorts of Biarritz? Country tweeds tailored to last a lifetime or button-through 'washing frocks' on sale in Oxford Street for 19s 11d?

They were all of these things and more as mass fashion – inspired as much by the cinema as by the couture salons of Paris – moved across the classes, and the ready-to-wear manufacturers and department stores responded to the growing need for fashionable dress at affordable prices. The history of fashion is not the smooth continuum fashion historians sometimes make it seem. Like most things, its progress is jerky. It goes in fits and starts. There are good periods and bad. Despite being overshadowed by the Twenties, the Thirties were not only a good period for fashion; they were an important one. They saw the strengthening of the shaky foundations of mass-market fashion which had been established in the previous decade; a phenomenal growth in fashion knowledge, stimulated by magazines which covered the whole social spectrum; the build-up of a consumer society in which clothes played a central role; the emergence of Hollywood not only as a powerful social and educative force but as tastemaker to the masses; and increased prosperity in a wider range of classes than ever before.

They also witnessed depression and penury; the rise of fascism and the totalitarian state; rural poverty and urban deprivation; hunger marches and mass unemployment; class estrangement and social indifference; extravagance and self-indulgence; homelessness, refugees and political and ethnic persecution.

Evening dress was worn by the top classes on both sides of the Atlantic. Here, at an English charity ball in 1938.

Like every other decade, they were socially and politically the best of times and the worst of times – and how you viewed them at the time depended on the position you held on the social pyramid. For those at the top, the rich and well-bred – and this was the last decade when the two could be taken as being virtually synonymous – the Thirties provided the final period of paradise. For them, things would never be so good again. Despite the instabilities of financial crashes and the Abdication – a body blow to the hierarchical system from which it recovered largely through the popularity of Queen Elizabeth's personality and appearance – the upper classes had much for which to be thankful. Their supply of servants, leisure and wealth seemed reasonably secure despite the increasing rumble of change.

Meredith Frampton's 1935 painting of a young woman shows all the hallmarks of upper-class elegance in the Thirties: understated, unadorned, but totally assured.

Formality was as important as decency. Even at the seaside many older men considered it 'fast' to be seen without a coat, tie and hat.

Although only the most benighted member of the upper classes could fail to see that the gradual entrenchments and realignments in society which had been forced on them since World War I would eventually destroy much that they still took for granted as, if not actually God-given, then certainly society-sanctioned, the way of life they had enjoyed for so long seemed, in essence at least, likely to continue. Everywhere, they were lulled by the comforting proofs of their continuity. The grounds and gardens they walked, frequently laid out 200 years earlier, could be expected to last for another 200. The taste and refinement displayed in their homes had been honed to perfection over many generations and needed little more than cosmetic tweaking to be kept abreast of the times. If they lost a minor country seat or two and had to abandon a town house to the cheque-books of developers, there was still sufficient left.

It was the women of this class who brought into existence the world of London couture, a growth which came to rapid fruition in the mid-Thirties. Society still circulated around the court in that the Season was the heart of the upper-class social calendar, even though many thought its quality was being eroded by 'outsiders' buying into what should be available only to breeding. In 1938, *Vogue* commented, 'In an age of social standards shifty as the sands of Araby...the system becomes more and more exploited...yammering hordes of social "racketeers" have introduced madness into method and turned a traditional practice into a flourishing industry.' It was understandable why parents wanted their daughters to have a season, even though the costs were daunting. Social sponsors – *Vogue*'s 'racketeers' – charged as much as £3,000 for taking on girls who otherwise would not have the vital backing for entrée to court in order to 'lead their feet...down the right and proper paths'.

But it was considered money well spent: 'From the moment her name first appears in the social columns,' *Vogue* went on, 'a débutante receives as much publicity and attention as a young film star. Milliners, hairdressers, photographers and beauty specialists compete for her custom with a steady stream of telephone calls, pre-paid telegrams and brochures. Dressmakers offer to dress her free, or nearly free...'

It was a world worth getting in on.

The bright young things of the Twenties had been displaced by the brightest of all young things – Edward VIII, who, as Prince of Wales, had become a world legend for his fashionable appearance and unstuffy approach to the protocol of dress. He had also achieved something else. Long before Wallis Simpson came upon the scene, he had made the idea of a royal fashion-maker popular not merely in Britain but in America too.

Thanks to him, it was the London fashion, the London season and the London attitudes that were influential. He gave the aristocratic style – which had been largely dormant since the previous Prince of Wales and the Edwardian period – a new, fashionable thrust. Everybody wanted to ape the upper classes.

There is nothing very different in that, of course – it has been the social leitmotiv for the last 500 years – but it had an important spin-off in fashion terms. It was in the Thirties that the accoutrements of upper-class male dressing became a fashion influence for the world. British tweeds and tailoring; English craftsmanship with leather; the traditional masculine bastions of hand-wrought shoes, saddles and luggage were what the world coveted. And they were coveted not only by men. Fashionable women the world over wanted English shoes, belts, scarves and handbags. The idea that you could tell a lady by her gloves, her shoes and her handbag came from one source: the perfection of the British upper-class – and country-based – life in the Thirties.

At the beginning of the decade, London had a plethora of court dressmakers. Often impressively skilled and with a remarkably high level of taste, they were famed for producing suitable creations for wear at formal royal occasions such as Presentations and Drawing Rooms. Wise to the minutiae of dress protocol and the many pitfalls for the uninformed, court dressmakers were an essential part of the upper-class social fabric. High on 'tone', they were low on originality because the formal and ritualised world for which they created was stultifyingly predictable and closed. They frequently copied the ideas which Paris seemed to produce with such prodigal ease but rarely reached the same levels of style. If some, such as the couturier Lucile or the tailoring firm of Creed – one of whose suits the spy Mata Hari chose to wear for her execution – or the royal dressmakers Handley-Seymour, stood above the crowd, most were no more than worthily pedestrian.

There was a demand for something better. A demand that came as much from wealthy international society women in North and South America as it did from their English counterparts: women in love with English 'class', longing to be the one chosen to dance with the Prince of Wales; women who wanted to be garbed in the authentic dress of the English lady;

Débutantes at Queen Charlotte's ball at the Dorchester, like peas in a very privileged pod.

The 'correct' accessories often cost more than the dress – here a bargain at just over £6.

women who turned to London to supplement the elegances of dress they already obtained from their couturiers in Paris. Their demands were fulfilled by the first – and in many respects only – wave of London couturiers, men who felt they could hold their heads high independent of what Paris was doing because they could present to the world a London look stronger than anything seen previously. It was a look based on well-tailored tweeds and romantic evening gowns – ingredients which have been the basis of London fashion ever since. As sharply tuned to the great outdoors as Paris is to the indoor pleasures of salon, dining room and boudoir, it reflected the English belief in the supremacy of country living and the national obsession with understatement, occasionally lightened by flashes of eccentricity, which the world perceived as uniquely British.

Nobody captured the nuances of British upper-class elegance better than Francis Marshall. These women wear furs and very chic hats for a charity matinee in 1936.

But if the London looks were strong, the confidence was not. One of the earliest couture houses to achieve an international reputation was not sufficiently assured even to use an English name. Lachasse – the chase – might well be a totally appropriate label for a house dedicated to sporting, country looks (albeit of the smartest kind) but it seems, in retrospect, slightly perverse for a dress house entirely British in 'feel' as well as in product to hide its lack of assurance behind a French title. Founded in 1927, with Digby Morton as its designer, Lachasse answered an upper-class need: a tweed suit which was neither country-rough nor city-slicker, something to be worn with equal ease at Goodwood or in the Ritz bar.

By answering a local need, Morton made an international classic. Nobody in Paris at this time was making a suit which so successfully mirrored

Few women could boast a boudoir as elegant as this, but make-up advances made the dressing table an increasingly enjoyable place to spend time.

the twin orbits of society life. Smart women around the world were soon ordering. By the time Morton was ready to open his own house in 1933, on the back of his success at Lachasse, the firm had made its mark. But it was Hardy Amies who made Lachasse a label which every smart North American shop felt it must carry throughout the Thirties and even into the Forties. He went to Lachasse, with no fashion training, in 1934. By the end of the decade he was considered one of London's finest couturiers, his designs combining English restraint with Gallic verve in a way that eluded most of his compatriots. In fact, although originally overshadowed by Norman Hartnell and later consigned to the elegant fashion backwater into which those who dress a Queen are automatically placed, Amies can be considered the most international of the British couturiers, in outlook as well as in approbation; second perhaps only to Captain Edward Molyneux, whose house was actually in Paris, although he was, like Morton, Irish.

Standing slightly apart but, in fact, the king pin of Thirties' London couture was Norman Hartnell, who came down from Cambridge, without finishing his studies but garlanded with high praise for his costume designs for the university's Footlights productions. He tried to find work with C. B. Cochrane, whose 'Revues' were the perfect showcase for a costume designer. He also approached Selfridges for work as a designer, but Gordon Selfridge could only suggest than that he went away and learned to draw. The society modiste Lucile published some of his drawings as her own, so he was forced to sue her: in all, few couturiers can have had so negative a start.

But Hartnell was determined. He originally set up on his own in 1924 with capital of £300. His romantic, rather theatrical clothes had an instant appeal, but he found that the snobbery of a Paris label meant more. Time and again, women looked, liked – and went to Paris in order to find something similar. He became so frustrated that he took his collection there in 1927, knowing that showing in the capital of elegance would give his name the kudos it required for an international profile. He repeated the experiment in 1930 and finally became accepted by North American couture customers as being on an equal footing with some of the good, but not the great, Paris couturiers.

It was in the Thirties that Hartnell became a world-famous name, although by no means a world-class couturier. His fame rested on his royal connection more than on his skills as a dress designer. Just as wealthy Americans had fallen in love with London via the Prince of Wales, so they had stayed in love – and wonder – as Wallis Simpson took centre stage by his side. Had she become Queen her almost clinically perfect elegance could well have made London a true rival to Paris. It would have been necessary for her to choose an English couturier as her official dressmaker. It is interesting to speculate on who it might have been. Certainly not Hartnell; possibly Edward Molyneux. His being based in Paris might have caused problems of protocol but, had the call come, it is easy to imagine the couturier moving his house to London rather than losing the kudos of designing for the Queen of England in days when such an honour automatically meant that every society woman would wish to be a customer of the 'royal' house. Of course, had she become Queen, that very fact would have sanctioned behaviour not entirely acceptable to the Establishment and Wallis Simpson might well have remained with the man who was to make her wedding dress, the Paris-based American Mainbocher, or even turned to any of the other top half-dozen names in Paris. All were, by her standards, superior to anyone working in London.

As it is, the king abdicated. George VI took over the throne and Elizabeth became Queen. It is easy to see her dress approach as a reaction to the 'fashion plate' perfection of the elegant Mrs Simpson. Certainly, the new Queen's individual style and oblique approach to the fashion conventions were more in keeping with the true spirit of upper-class English dress than the Simpson look could ever be. Whereas the Queen's way of dressing was understood and admired by the majority of her class – who were neither internationally nor fashionably inclined – the Simpson style was understood by and appealed to perhaps fewer than 100 women in London society. Although they dressed stylishly, using Paris rather than London as their source, and stood out elegantly against the slightly eccentric fancy dress appearance of the shire-based Englishwoman who so enjoyed Hartnell's fantasies, they were not typical.

The man who said, 'I am more than partial to the jolly glitter of sequins' was no believer in understated elegance. Hartnell's approach could never be considered minimalist. But his deep love of the theatre – which frequently led him into lapses of taste and made most of his collections rather too flamboyant for the truly elegant woman – made him the ideal man to dress the Queen. Royal dress must never be pedestrian. It requires a style outside the prevailing conventions of modishness. It must, in fact, reflect current fashion as little as possible if it is to retain its dignity. A Queen cannot dress so much in the fashion that a picture of her ten – or even five – years later will cause people to smile and think her old-

No elegant wardrobe was complete without its furs: sable, mink, nutria, Persian lamb or a fox-fur stole.

fashioned. That is why Queens require their own style. Queen Elizabeth realised this and, in choosing Hartnell as her dress-maker, picked a man who understood how to dress a woman who, at every public appearance, is treading the stage, in the limelight, being observed by an audience. Hartnell succeeded remarkably well. Pictures of Queen Elizabeth from the Thirties and Forties look dated, of course, but they rarely look old-fashioned.

Above all, her clothes never make her appear risible. She comes across the decades to us with both dignity and style. This is a testimony to the choice of an approach within which she and Hartnell could work consistently and the way in which they mixed what very quickly became the Queen's 'trademarks'. The fluidity of soft material and floating silhouettes; the absence of strong or strident colour; the decorative detailing – including the sequins of which *both* were very fond – are all still valid today. Public attitudes have changed only one aspect of Queen Elizabeth's dress: the fur trims and ostrich feathers which were a feature in the Thirties – often as a compliment to countries of the Empire – are no longer acceptable. Otherwise, her clothes seem perfectly attuned to the theatrical role of the position demanded of her.

Norman Hartnell adjusts actress Florence Desmond's wedding dress for the benefit of news cameras in 1936.

But such success does not make Hartnell a great couturier. Amies was greater and so was Victor Stiebel, the South African who opened his house in Bruton Street in 1932. But 'pecking orders' are irrelevant. None of the couturiers working in London was as great as their top French counterparts. And they knew it. Was it a manifestation of a collective inferiority complex or a belief that only in unity is strength that in 1935 the most famous London names, excluding Hartnell, joined together to show to the American press and buyers under the banner of the Fashion Group of Great Britain? The group consisted of the young Turks – Amies at Lachasse, Stiebel and Morton – alongside established but not cutting-edge houses such as Busvine and Glenny, both popular for their immaculate tailoring; Lydia Moss; Motley, the three sisters who eventually concentrated on theatrical costumes; Teddy Tinling, who later specialised in tennis dress; Aage Thaarup, who became the Queen's milliner; Allan Solbey for jerseys; Benbaron for accessories and Fortnum & Mason for shoes.

This group hoped not to take on the might of Paris but to convince Americans that London had a separate fashion

Wallis Simpson, a world-class fashion leader, wearing Schiaparelli's famous lobster dress, inspired by Salvador Dali.

identity and was able to produce things to a standard not found elsewhere in the world: the quality of man-tailored suits; the best tweed in the world; the fine craftsmanship of leather work. And they succeeded, to a degree.

A joint fashion show was reported in the *Transvaal & Johannesburg Star* as strongly reflecting 'the Queen's preference for British-made goods. The designers used almost entirely throughout British material, including ostrich feathers and much wool.' The same show, held in the Mayfair garden of the Mirabelle – for the third consecutive season – was criticised because each member was permitted to parade only one outfit as a taster for his full collection, available by appointment in his showroom. The American trade newspaper *Women's Wear Daily* commented, logically if tartly, 'Since there were so few models it was difficult to gather definite style trends as featured by British designers.' Could the reason be that there were no definitive style trends which could have given London fashion a unique personality? Was London fashion basically only a question of fine material and good workmanship? If so, no matter how much it might please fashionable English women, it could never be anything more than peripheral to international women who could dress wherever they wished. For many fashionable women, the most important persons in the couture house were not the couturiers but the cutters and fitters. They set the standard of a house and, although Busvine's Louis Le Carlier was exceptional, no London house could compete with the likes of M. Fernaud at Molyneux, M. François at Creed or Schiaparelli's tailor, René, all of whom worked in Paris.

The designers knew that regardless of their attempts to attract a world clientèle their bread and butter depended on their ability to please English women above all else. And here they were well served by the publicity provided in the pages of *Vogue* and *Harper's Bazaar*, the premier fashion and society magazines of the time. Both threw their considerable kudos behind the London designers, reporting their shows with the same enthusiasm and at the same length with which they covered those in Paris.

The fashion map of London was on a village scale. Nearly every major fashion house was within a five-minute walk of Berkeley Square and the most fashionable thoroughfare was undoubtedly Bruton Street, peppered on either side with dress establishments, including Hartnell. The women who made up London high society hardly needed the pages of advice and information found in the glossies. Lunch at the Ritz; tea at Claridges or a cocktail at the Berkeley and they had seen and heard everything of note. Where *Vogue* and *Harper's Bazaar* were invaluable was to the women who, although not part of the international smart set and with never a hope of dancing with the Prince of Wales, nevertheless saw it as a duty and privilege of their social position to dress not just smartly but fashionably.

The upper middle-class woman – wife of the gentry landowner, the circuit judge, the barrister, senior consultant or stockbroker – wanted to be fashionable not merely in dress but also in attitude. For her, the glossies were essential reading. *Harper's Bazaar*'s editorial, 'The Pulse of Fashion' was compulsive but so were its social observations. From them, she learned the right holiday destinations. Not just Deauville, Menton and Le Touquet but 'the smaller sun-set jewelled places' such as Ste Maxine, Bendol and La Ciotat, as well as 'the paradise – Juan-les-Pins'. She read the monthly comments of the Honourable Mrs

The Queen was in mourning at the time of the State visit to Paris in 1939. Hartnell created a sensational all-white wardrobe for her.

1939: Cecil Beaton's photographs of the Queen, taken in the gardens of Buckingham Palace, were unashamedly romantic.

James Rodney and Lady Sybell Lygon and believed them because the writers were not only knowledgeable, they were ladies.

The power of the 'lady' in Thirties society was immense. Regardless of breeding and background, every woman in Britain – and much further afield – wished to be taken for one. Her distinguishing characteristics were easy to recognise, if hard to emulate. She was gracious, refined, strong but not assertive, moral, caring and aware of her debt to society. Her appearance, understated and smart, although never gaudy, was crucial. She looked to Queen Elizabeth as the perfection of the type and turned from Mrs Simpson as being merely wealthy enough to be so fashionable that she teetered dangerously close to the edge: that social nemesis labelled 'nouveau riche'.

James Gunn's portraits of 'Pauline' explored his sitter's personality and mood as much through her dress as through her expression.

Breeding was all to the British, who found the influx of stylish upper-class American women stimulating and amusing, but could never take them and their very modern way of life entirely seriously. The reason was that American money seemed so rarely inherited and, no matter what beauties it bought, always came with the most lethal of all stings in the tail for the British: it was openly and obviously derived from trade and industry – even, heaven forbid, from a down-market chain store like Woolworths.

But the well-bred, well-off British woman realised the importance of her appearance just as much as any American heiress did. To be incorrectly dressed was for her a betrayal of her class – the most hallowed of all things in which she believed. But 'correct' dress was not in her eyes necessarily highly fashionable dress. Far from it. She understood and followed the nuances of taste more than the vagaries of fashion. What was 'done' or 'not done' in dress was infinitely more important than being in the very latest style. In fact, an over-fashionable appearance was often seen as vulgar – a sort of flaunting of privilege and wealth which, with the canny instinct for survival which has prevented the rolling of tumbrels in England, the upper classes have always known was unwise, if not dangerous. Exotic creatures like Mrs Rita d'Acosta Lydig, who had her shoes made from medieval fabrics with shoe trees cut from the wood of seventeenth-century violins and carried them everywhere in Russian leather trunks, could never have come from the English upper classes. Such extravagant blooms may well be appreciated – 'so

amusing' – but they were not to be emulated by an English-born lady.

Few upper-class Englishwomen bothered with a couturier, whether in Paris or London. Instead, they patronised the grand court dressmakers such as Reville and Rossiter, favourites of Queen Mary, and the lesser fry found in tiny showrooms or upstairs rooms in the side streets of Mayfair who could produce much the same effect for half the cost. For 'serious' clothes they frequently turned to men, having their suits and winter coats – meant to last for many seasons – tailored by the craftsmen who produced the same outfits for their fathers, husbands and brothers. Certainly, their famed 'sensible' shoes were made on the lasts of shoemakers who had, for generations, catered largely for a male clientèle.

Not all such craftsmen were in London. Many country-based women employed the services of tailors and shoemakers in their own county town – as did their husbands – especially if they were remote from London. And, for most of their other clothes requirements there were the dressmakers, the backbone of fashion for most women.

It is not easy for us to imagine how important the dressmaker was in the Thirties because today she has been totally usurped by good quality – even 'designer' – ready-to-wear clothing, readily available. In the Thirties, couturiers made clothes for individual customers. They had no ready-to-wear ranges, although some sold sports and 'fun' clothes, not made on their premises, in shops attached to their salons – the very earliest attempts at designer boutiques. The people who satisfied the demand for quality made-to-measure clothing in the latest style were the dressmakers. Usually trading under a grand-sounding but entirely fictitious French name – Madame Renée; Monsieur Jacques – they were often people who had trained with a couturier before setting up on their own. Scattered in their thousands across the country, in the cities they were nearly always Jewish, frequently refugees and often brilliantly perceptive when it came to understanding and copying the feel as well as the line of a new look. Even in country towns, they were always highly competent and just as informed about the latest fashion developments.

Although only the rich could afford grand perfumes from Paris, any woman could enjoy the mass-market Californian Poppy.

Their information came from the glossy magazines. The grandest would subscribe to *L'Officiel de la Couture*, the French fashion magazine first published in 1921 and dedicated to recording the very best of French couture. It concentrated entirely on Paris and gave exposure to French houses – great and small – and their milliners and accessory-makers on a monthly basis. Read by only the most obsessive of fashionable women, it was the Bible for the trade. *L'Officiel* was unique in its single-minded devotion to French couture, but it was not the only magazine to which dressmakers and tailors could turn. *Vogue* produced a separate pattern book, tied to the main magazine, ostensibly for home dressmakers but also invaluable to the trade, especially those at the bottom end, for the way in which it adapted and simplified the current trend so that any competent dressmaker could cope, professional or not. Again, it is difficult to imagine now, but in the Thirties virtually every middle-class woman was a needlewoman of some level of skill. Having learned to sew at school or at the hand of their nanny, most were capable of taking a pattern – if not *Vogue*, then *Weldon's* or *Butterick* – and producing an acceptable cotton dress for summer or a woollen skirt for winter wear. Such patterns were available across the social spectrum of women's magazines, from the grandest monthly to the 3d weekly. Newspapers also carried patterns. Some publications offered,

High drama and romance combine in this theatrical evening gown from Molyneux's 1938 Summer Collection, photographed by Horst.

for a nominal sum, to take the risk out of home dressmaking by providing a cutting-out and making-up service.

But for the lady, *Vogue*'s pattern book was peripheral. One of her favourite magazines was *Woman's Journal*, with its monthly cover portrait of similar ladies, which offered a much wider menu than high fashion and commentary on high society. Not that fashion was neglected. In addition to 'muslin models cut in Paris (5/- each, post free)' and 'hand-cut paper patterns (1/6 each, post free)' cut to the individual's measurements, it chose the more wearable of couture models for its artists to draw each month. These illustrations were taken to the dressmaker to be adapted as the basis of a wardrobe in the spirit of the top mode without spending a fortune.

And, of course, there were the department stores, all of whom had 'model gown' departments and a team of designers and tailors to make clothes on an individual basis. Fortnum & Mason, Harrods and Debenham & Freebody were favourites with women from the shires because they created their own models, sold direct line-for-line copies of Paris originals and stocked the fashionable labels from the top end of the ready-to-wear lines. As *The Times* pointed out: 'The important London stores are the real source of fashion buying to the majority of women, having elegant dress departments where they find an infinite variety, different price grades and all the sizes and colourings.' For tailored items Matita, Sumrie, Dorville, Hebe and Spectator Sports were all acceptable to a lady in too much of a hurry to visit a tailor. These firms used the best materials – with a heavy emphasis on Scottish wool and tweed – and tailored them to the highest standards.

In order to make their quality clear to the sort of customer for which they were catering, ready-to-wear firms and 'top people's' stores often featured society women in their advertisements: Matita had the Countess Bosdari travelling north on the Royal Highlander in one of its tweed travelling ensembles; Fortnum & Mason showed Mrs Philip Kindersley looking 'deliciously cool and utterly spring-like in one of our newest Ready-to-Wear suits ... Price 8½ guineas'. There were many more.

To the middle-class woman – wife of a country doctor, lawyer or an officer in the services – the top stores often seemed unnecessarily expensive and they were more inclined to patronise Marshall & Snelgrove, Bourne & Hollingsworth, Dickins & Jones or Robinson & Cleaver for bought clothes. In fact, this was the class which relied most heavily on a dressmaker; the class for whom magazines – including august ones such as *Vogue* – featured lengthy articles on fabrics, their colours, patterns and textures, as well as advertisements from manufacturers such as British Celanese, Jacqmar, Tootal and Edinburgh weavers.

The average middle-class woman in the Thirties possessed a depth of dressmaking knowledge totally lost to her counterpart today. She was not only informed about materials – spending many absorbing hours in the fabric departments found in all major stores as well as The Needlewoman in Regent Street or the specialist shops in Bond Street – she also understood about buttons, belts and all the other things which went to making a good-quality outfit.

Above all, she understood about fit, as any person does who has actually had a garment made to measure – a perfectly normal thing in the Thirties but increasingly rare today. By going to a good fitter and making the experience an active, learning one rather than merely standing passively whilst fitter and assistant worked on and around her, a woman was able to pick up the tricks of the trade so that she could instruct her local 'woman' and ensure that she did her job correctly. Many women found the occasional extra expense of going to a West End model house repaid itself many times over in pitfalls avoided at a local level.

But the costs of such visits alarmed some. In January 1939, *Eve's Journal* published 'A sisterly essay for frightened people' in order to allay fears of huge bills: 'I couldn't, darling, not a Mayfair dressmaker! You never get out under at least 40 pounds – and think of all the fittings. Hours and hours and hours, and unless you're *terribly* society, nobody looks at you,' it cried, playing devil's advocate before demolishing the prejudice with a few facts.

Two instances will suffice. Lachasse preferred two fittings and a finished fitting, but could 'make do with two fittings only for out-of-towners and will charge only 13 guineas for a plain tweed suit'.

Paris at its most elegant, drawn by Bouché in 1939: jackets, bustles and bows by Schiaparelli (left), Rochas (centre) and Francevramant.

Madame Destin of Grosvenor Street, 'who was once with Chanel and still works in the Chanel tradition – slick and unfussy, but very, very feminine, can manage with only one fitting and provides a special service for country women. She is prepared to send drawings and even dresses to country clients in order that they might choose over the weekend. Thus, a frock made to one's own measurements requires only one trip to London.' The prices were considered competitive too: a woollen day dress cost 12 guineas, an evening dress up to 20 guineas. In this, *Eve's Journal* was being disingenuous. Girls in the garment trade at this time were earning 12s 6d per week, in some cases for a seventy hour stint. To be able to afford a one-fitting day dress from Madame Destin would require over two months' work at such a rate. Although no working woman ever crossed her doorstep, of course, it is precisely because West End houses cost so much that women with considerably more spending power than the garment workers sought out their own dressmakers.

The long silhouette of the Thirties had reached suburbia by 1935, as had gas-mask mania.

A middle-class woman's dressmaker was seen as her greatest ally. She was also her best kept secret, not someone to be shared with a friend. The cynical society joke was that a woman would rather lose her husband to a friend than lose her dressmaker, a good replacement being infinitely easier to find for the former than the latter. Regardless of her level of proficiency, a dressmaker was as essential a part of the middle-class life as a good cook and, like one's dentist or doctor, once found, was not lightly changed.

Of course, millions of women in the Thirties made all their own – and their children's – clothes, except for 'special occasion' items. This is especially true of the group most characteristic of the age: the suburban housewives whose well-ordered lives ringed every city in the land. Between the two wars, four million suburban dwellings – mainly semi-detached – were erected in the South East. They swallowed up over 60,000 acres per year but, more than that, they housed a new sub-class which they had created. We find it easy to patronise the suburbs now, but in the Thirties they were genuinely believed by reformers and intellectuals to be part of a Brave New World and the attitudes found in them were seen – not entirely incorrectly – as the trailblazers of the future. Inevitably, suburban women had a considerable impact on fashion. They were a newly enfranchised market needing to buy in order to 'place' themselves in their new environment. The wives of clerks, school teachers, minor civil servants and even shopkeepers, they had jumped a class barrier from the

upper working and artisanal class into the lower middle. If they weren't particularly well educated, at least their husbands had normally obtained qualifications and their sons and daughters would be first-generation university students in the Fifties, so they held a pivotal position.

The suburban women read magazines as primers for behaviour. They learned how to care for their homes and cook for their families by reading *Good Housekeeping*, which made a feature of publishing family budgets to teach them how to manage their finances and avoid going into debt. They discovered how to dress cheaply but smartly from *Women & Beauty* and *Woman's Weekly*, depending on their intellectual level and the money at their disposal. From *Woman's Own*, founded in 1932 as 'the new big-value weekly for the up-to-date wife', they learned the nuances of their new status, whilst its rival, *Woman*, which appeared in 1937, promised to help them 'in every way possible' with 'reliable advice on almost every question under the sun'. They learned how to make their own clothes through the 'Bestway' Fashion books for home dressmakers: coats and suits; washing frocks; skirts, jackets and blouses, all at 6d each.

Magazines taught them the elements of taste, as their securely middle-class editorial writers saw it: 'In certain fundamentals your clothes must be conventionally planned to show a sense of discrimination...the true sign of a cultured woman... You will never be led into "artistic" eccentricities...you will avoid everything that is described as "quaint". In cut and line your clothes must be impeccable... of course, you stand and walk well.' *Woman & Beauty* was even more fundamentally didactic. 'Is your handkerchief clean this morning?' it asked. 'Do you ever enter a restaurant with a cigarette in your mouth? Are you perfectly certain that none of your shoes wants heeling?'

The quality of make-up improved consistently through out the Thirties, at all price levels.

Between all the admonitions was the fashion knowledge to enable the reader to dress correctly for her new social role. Even more important as an educational tool were the advertisements, essential guides for newcomers to a consumer society. Arris Cream Deodorant, 'Personality' turtle oil soap, Amani wave sets at 1s 3d and the ubiquitous Californian Poppy perfume and make-up range were the things to pop into Boot's for. Everything a woman could require to make her refined and ladylike, someone of whom the Queen – whom every suburban woman adored – might be proud, could be found, advertised and explained in the

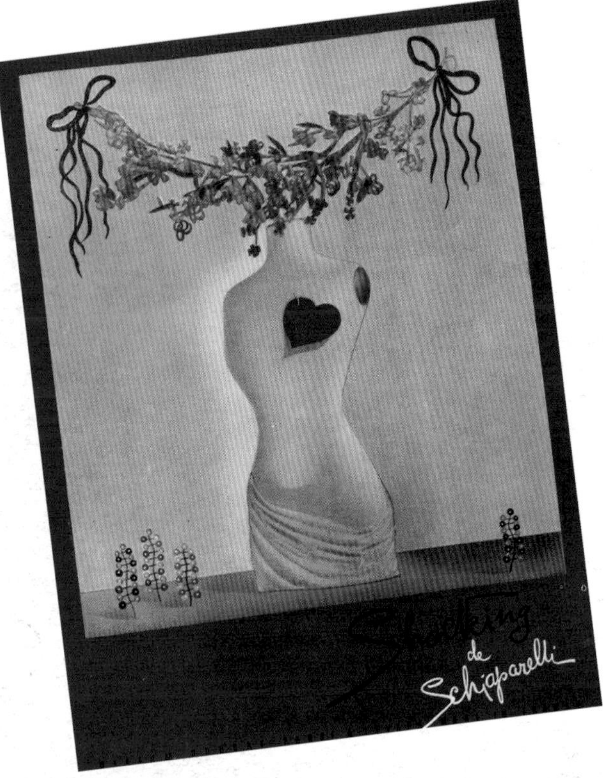

The bright pink box and a bottle based on Mae West's figure guaranteed Schiaparelli's scent 'Shocking' a best-seller's notoriety.

women's magazines and the columns increasingly devoted to middle-class fashion in the popular newspapers. If the backbone of the country was the established middle classes, then the suburban lower middle classes were to prove equally valuable in the Thirties, not only as underpinning but also as pointers to the new attitudes to come.

One of the pleasures of suburban life was clothes, making and buying. One of the joys was shopping, especially for those who lived on the outskirts of London. Cheap rail fares and the convenience of the underground made a day in town perfectly feasible. Just as Knightsbridge and Mayfair were the shopping areas for the rich and well born, so Oxford Street and Regent Street catered for the suburban housewife. Lunch at Lyons (poached egg on toast for 6½d); teas at the Cumberland, serenaded by a Hungarian gypsy band; Peter Robinson, Robinson & Cleaver and John Lewis; C & A's Under £1 department for dresses, blouses and skirts and, for an extra 'splash', the Better Dress department where an embroidered dress and jacket could be had for 39s 11d. It seemed a consumer's paradise. As often as not a matinee at the pictures was squeezed in as well. And this was probably the most educative influence of all. Hollywood introduced glamour to the most humdrum of lives. It brought sophistication to every suburban back door. It idealised the consumer-orientated, middle-class urban lifestyle as a separate and perfectly acceptable cultural force, apart from upper-class grandeur but accepting many of its tenets. Above all, it made America chic for millions of people who would only ever know of that country what they saw on the aptly named 'silver screen'.

Myrna Loy, Katharine Hepburn, William Powell and Fred MacMurray wisecracked their way through a world of sizzling sophistication – kitchens, bathrooms and patios of a level of luxury undreamed of by most British cinemagoers. And their clothes! Made to the highest levels of couture, of the richest materials – these were the days when, if the script specified a sable coat, a sable coat it was, with no imitations accepted – and designed by costume designers often way ahead of Paris in understanding what the public liked, they were not only an eye-opener, they were an ideal to be sought after.

It is undoubtedly true that, for the majority of women, Hollywood fashion was more immediate, vibrant and accessible than anything which came from the salons of the couturiers. It was also much more influential, even if the names of the great designers – Walter Plunkett, who created the costumes for *Gone With the Wind*; Edith Head, who dressed Mae West in *She Done Him Wrong*, and

Orry-Kelly, Bette Davis' favourite – were totally unknown. The suit for Joan Crawford in *Humoresque* designed by Adrian, or the Travis Banton evening gown worn by Marlene Dietrich in *The Devil Is a Woman* were seen by millions whilst a photograph in a fashion magazine reached only a few thousand readers. Mass-manufacturers realised this, picked up a film star's new way with a collar or a belt, and put it into production immediately, knowing that the world was so star-struck that anything worn by the screen goddesses would sell to women everywhere.

For many dressmakers, the twice-weekly trip to the cinema was a form of training as well as a pleasure. A well-known London PR consultant fondly recalls her aunt, a Jewish dressmaker who lived in Maida Vale. 'Her kitchen was always indescribable. Two sewing machines, huge irons, half-made dresses, boxes of buttons and *always* swelteringly hot and full of cigarette smoke. It seemed an absolute tip to me but auntie always seemed to know *exactly* where everything was. The front room was different. Kept immaculate. It had a huge cheval mirror. The customers were fitted in there and I remember they used to bring copies of *Picturegoer* to show my aunt the fashions of the stars they wanted her to copy. And my aunt saw all the latest films. Her great love was Norma Shearer. She thought her the most elegant.'

It was the cinema, far more than anything worn by a society lady in the pages of *Vogue*, that impressed the average suburban shopper. She scoured Oxford Street or her local high street shops for the sort of clothes worn by her favourite stars and, more often that not, found them, usually at a price that she could manage to afford.

Marlene Dietrich in *The Devil Is a Woman*, a lodestar of glamour in clothes made to the highest levels of couture, regardless of cost.

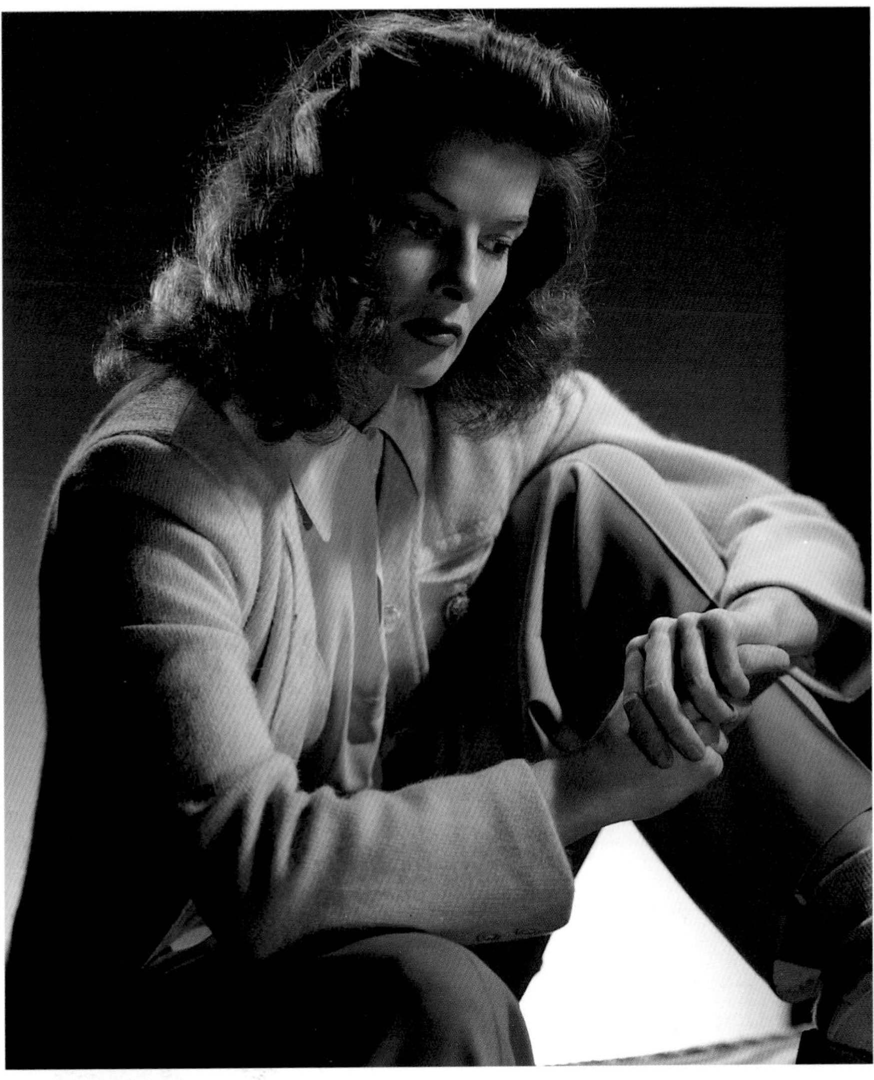

Hollywood stars were icons of style in the Thirties and their fashion influence was immense. The casual, sporty look of Katharine Hepburn was a precursor of what was to come. She took items from the male wardrobe and made them not just feminine but also sexy.

No wonder the suburban woman looked back sadly at her working-class sisters for whom such a life was still out of the question. The class system in the Thirties was remarkably homogenous and it was probably the last time when all classes felt that they knew their place, were more or less happy to be there – and dressed the part accordingly. The opportunity to do so was more equally distributed than at any previous time in history, even though the gaps between the classes were, by today's standards, vast and, indeed, by the tenets of the times, almost unbridgeable. It wasn't merely a question of money. It was also a matter of what society sanctioned as correct dress for each class – and, by society, we must not imagine some remote and lordly cabal of taste-makers sitting in judgement on high. Each and every class had its ideas of suitability. It proclaimed its own standards, which were not to be transgressed. By the late Thirties, for example, high society glossy magazines increasingly featured trousers for leisure wear in which they were following the lead of some of the more sophisticated of the current film actresses. The middle classes – traditionally the prudish underbelly of British society – were much more circumspect in what and where trousers might be worn without breaking the bounds of propriety. The working classes were much less ambivalent. Trousers dictated by the exigencies of work – on the land, in dirty factories – were acceptable. Socially, especially in rural areas, they were seen as the dress of the immoral woman, hated and feared as a threat in a society based on the sanctity of marriage and the family unit.

As one woman living in the North East at the time told me, 'No decent woman wore trousers. It just wasn't allowed.' That usually meant that it was unacceptable, above all, to the working-class male – at least, as far as his wife, daughter or girlfriend was concerned. And it must be remembered that whether working, middle or upper class, how the English male viewed female dress at this time was largely how it would be. Few women had the financial or emotional strength to defy the paterfamilias who, as breadwinner, considered his role as that of moral, social and, indeed, fashion arbiter for the women in his care.

The female position in all classes before World War II was almost entirely subservient to the male. Unmarried women were largely ruled by the whim of others – usually their parents, of course, and normally their father, even though his rulings were most frequently conveyed by proxy through their mother. The list of prohibitions was a modern ten commandments, multiplied a hundred times. And they *were* prohibitions, each one beginning with 'Thou shalt not'. In fact, each social class in the Thirties was largely endogamous, concerning itself primarily with the reactions of its own fellows when judging and finding levels of acceptability in behaviour – especially those to do with dress and its natural partner, sex. There was also – certainly within the working classes – a further complication in that what might be acceptable in a city would be less so in a small town and totally beyond the pale in a village or hamlet. For the working and lower middle classes the prohibitions were more to do with behaviour than dress, for the simple reason that opportunities to transgress in the latter were limited because they had so few clothes.

Hardly surprisingly. In the mid-Thirties, a barrister was earning

The glamour of film costume had its effect even on Paris. This 1938 Alix evening gown, photographed by Horst, could have stepped straight from the screen.

A drawing by Willaumez of a Chanel evening gown. Lace bodice and skirt in stiff slipper satin are topped by a splendid panache.

on average £1000 a year, a train driver £258 and a senior member of the clergy £400; an agricultural worker took home about £89 per year and a shop assistant just over £100. And there were many working for even less than that, quite apart from the considerable numbers of unemployed. Keeping decently, let alone smartly, dressed was a constant battle. Market stalls selling shoddy goods at low prices were the most common resort for hard-pressed working-class women, although whatever they bought apparently cheap was in fact expensive because it had such a short life. The average wardrobe of the poorer woman was scant indeed. There was rarely a repetition of items. One of each item, except underwear, and lots of gaps: a coat, but no mackintosh; a scarf, but only one; a little sentimental jewellery and, for decency, a hat. Many were hand-me-downs and had to be cared for so that they could eventually be passed on to someone else in the family. From sheer necessity virtually all working-class women made their clothes and those of their family. At least material was cheap and plentiful. For suits, jackets and coats, they saved up or bought on 'tick' for a small weekly payment. Keeping properly shod was often possible only by this method. One of the most telling remarks was made to me by a woman who said that when she went into the forces the most luxurious thing for her was 'to have a pair of shoes that had never been worn before. They were as hard as hell and I was crippled for weeks but it didn't matter. I was so proud. Nobody else's foot had ever been in those shoes before me.'

The battle for boots was probably the biggest dress problem for the poor. Essential, expensive, but often poorly made, they soon needed repairing. Every working-class man owned a last to keep the family's shoes in reasonable shape as cheaply as possible.

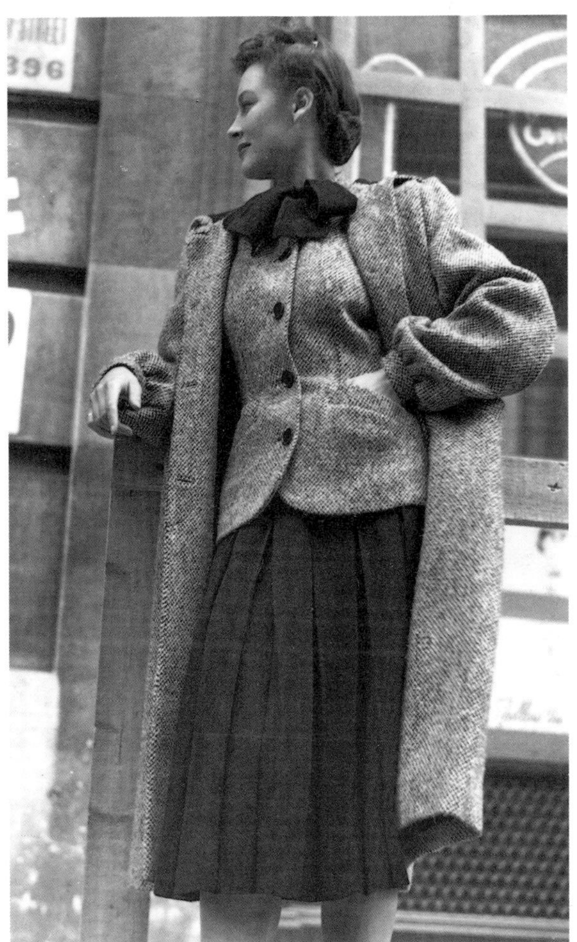

Tweeds for town by Dorville. Practical, efficient and smart, this look was not likely to 'date' quickly.

Of course, at this level clothes are a matter of expediency, not choice, and fashion does not enter the equation. The grand couturier might as well have been on a different planet for all his relevance to the inner-city poor and the breadline existence of most who worked on the land.

HARRY McDONALD
VOGUE DESIGN 8273—ALSO SHOWN ON PAGE 13

Vogue Pattern Book brought a fashionable appearance to women who could not afford couture creation. Most dressmakers could cope with a dress like this.

Things were even worse in France but that did not stop Paris fighting for fashion supremacy. Like London, it used everything it could to get publicity. When King George VI and Queen Elizabeth visited France in 1938, they were given, on behalf of the children of France, as a gift for the young princesses, a collection of dolls with a 300-piece wardrobe designed by the top names in Paris, including Lanvin, Patou, Paquin, Piquet, Vionnet and Worth; hats by Agnès, Reboux and Suzy; furs by Weil and jewellery by Cartier.

On 10 August that year, history was made with a live broadcast of *Vogue*'s report on the Paris opening fashion shows, transmitted to New York and relayed from there. Paris was beset by contenders. London was especially keen to break into the lucrative American market. Desperate to keep interest high, the Fashion Group televised the September 1938 London shows from Radiolympia, described by the *Daily Herald* as featuring 'the latest fashions in dresses, furs, jewellery and hats totalling in value over £50,000...no fewer than 120 mannequins featuring some of the loveliest débutantes' including Tania Sharman, 'trained and groomed for two years to be the finest television model in the world'.

The Fashion Group began to produce a quarterly magazine, aimed mainly at the trade, in an attempt to keep resolve high and in the hope that splits might be avoided. Unity was extolled at every opportunity, although criticism was allowed by the Group's President, Lady Maureen Stanley, wife of the President of the Board of Trade. The first woman to lecture at the Sorbonne, which she did in French, the *Quarterly* described her as a 'very modern person, compact of energy and versatility'. The Group needed both. Low tariffs were making it easy for American manufacturers to sell their goods in England and the Americans were encouraging their own designers to produce the high-fashion clothes which were currently being provided by English couturiers. Trade prospects did not look good as Europe slid inexorably towards war. The *Express & Star* summed up the attitude of most Londoners when it reported, 'Talking advance fashion seems futile at the time of writing, when the grim spectre of European conflict hangs menacingly over our heads.'

The symbolism of this Lee Miller picture might seem obvious today, but in 1939 what it said was only partly confined to fashion.

1 : 3000000

CHAPTER 2

COSTUMES OF WAR

LEFT: Poignant partings at Paddington. ABOVE: Happy hellos for new recruits.

Everyone in Britain knew that it was coming but few could imagine, even as late as 1939, what it would bring. One of the least expected results of the declaration of war was the way in which the civilian life of the country was so quickly taken over and ordered by the government. Regulations and restrictions seemed even at the time to be draconian, verging on the unanswerable rule of the totalitarian state. Yet so powerful was the wave of patriotism that few of the government's edicts produced anything more noticeable than the tendency to grumble which had been noted by perceptive foreign visitors over at least the past hundred years as a national characteristic and safety valve of the British.

The majority of people believed that Hitler must be stopped, regardless of cost. No privations, inconveniences or personal irritations could be allowed to stand in the way of the war effort. For men, the decision was easy, having been taken out of their hands with mobilisation. For women, a much greater act of will, a much greater form of courage, was called upon when the decision to be involved, the decision to play an *active* part in the war effort, was made.

In war, the traditional female role is a holding one. The preservation of hearth and home; the continuation of law and order and the conservation of resources have been the woman's lot since the Crusades and even further back, beyond Greece and Rome, to the very first war ever embarked upon by disputatious tribesmen. World War II was no exception. As the call-up swung into action, women's magazines backed the movement with a series of clarion calls to that most powerful of social aphrodisiacs in time of civil danger, the call of duty. The *Vogue* 'leader' for 20 September 1939, headed 'Power Behind the Throne' gave its readers not only a role but a figurehead with whom to identify. At this time Queen Elizabeth was probably the most popular Queen Consort in history. Women of all classes believed in her goodness, wisdom and strength. The whole country felt indebted to her for the highly significant part she had played in steadying the situation – seen as one of great danger for the country and for the Royal Family – after the Abdication. *Vogue* rightly identified her as the talismanic figure who could help women bear the sadness, bewilderment, loneliness and frustration which it and the government knew were to be their lot in the months and possibly years to come.

The formula which was propounded was simple but sound: the Queen supports the King; we women must similarly support our men whether they are in the services or doing vital war work out of uniform.

Join now

A·T·S or W·A·A·F

Recruiting posters made service dress look smart and sophisticated.

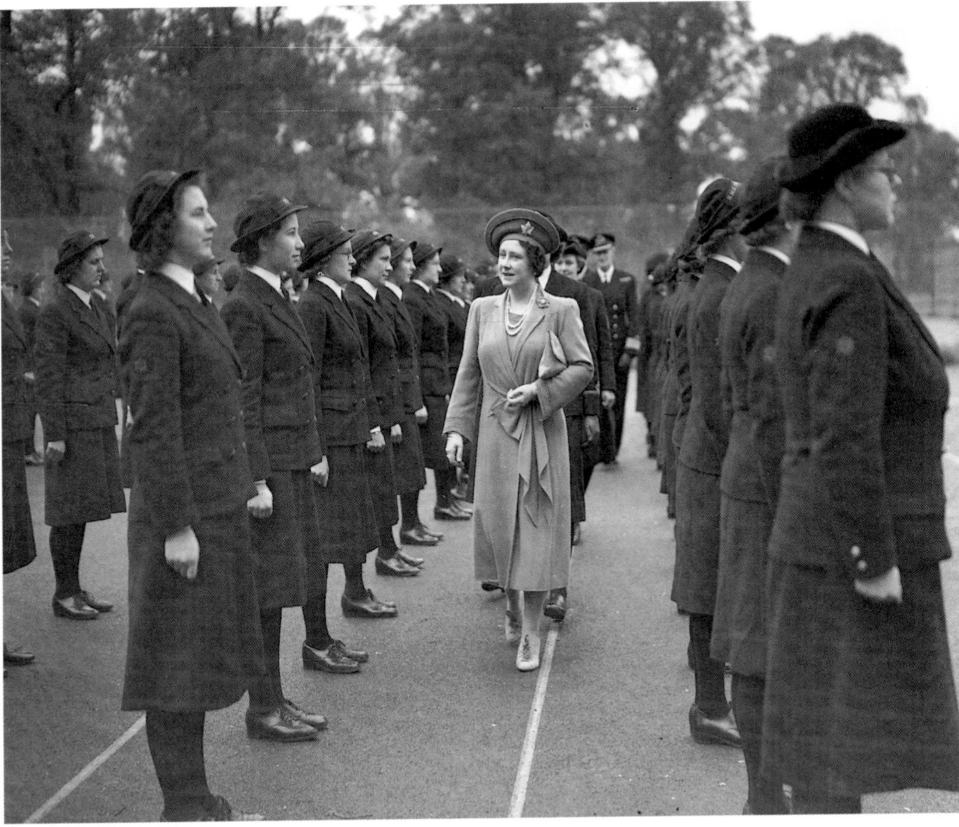

Although never seen in uniform, the Queen's appearance, especially her shoulders and hats, echoed elements of military dress.

And, to do so, we, the women of Britain, must be strong, undeviating and courageous. As the leader talked of the 'inevitable and tremendous changes in civil life', it took care to include women in the drama and history of it all, knowing that to keep them on the sidelines would cause alienation which, when the difficulties really began, could result in apathy and worse.

'For those who are attached to the auxiliary reserves of the fighting forces,' *Vogue* said, 'the way is clear: they are under military discipline and must obey orders.' It was the rest – the vast majority of the country's female population – whom *Vogue* felt were in need of stiffening and guidance. The piece reads strangely to modern eyes, as if women were being patronised, not by men in government, which they could expect, but by others of their own sex. There is a feeling that *Vogue* imagined the country full of women crouching like frightened rabbits, ready to run at the first sign of danger; women who would panic without the presence of their men to stabilise them; women whose heads must be filled with a series of ruses to act as placebos. Bearing in mind the undoubted level of sophistication achieved by the average *Vogue* reader, some of the suggestions seem not only simplistic but almost a joke.

'Learn to cook,' the magazine suggested, adding – on a note of expediency – that 'professional cooks will soon be spirited away'. It continued, 'Sew or knit something, preferably not too complicated. This is not to put your dressmaker out of work but to give you something to do in hours of waiting.' The advice becomes increasingly unlikely: 'If you are fond of bridge, darts or any mild diversion...get your company together...and play a quiet game...' 'Learn – or re-learn – to play some musical instrument. If you haven't a piano... try the recorder, mouth organ, or accordion...'

At the same time, *Harper's Bazaar* was trying in its own way to stabilise flighty womanhood. In a feature called 'Fashion as Usual', published in the autumn of 1939, the magazine was at pains to suggest that the best way to overcome wartime fears and depressions was to continue life as much as possible in the way it had been for over a decade. There was an air of unreality about it all: 'The war girl of 1939, practical and ready for anything in Debenham & Freebody tweed-knit slacks,' one caption read, whilst an article began with 'The moment the sirens go, I make for the Ritz...'

Parachute making was vital war work for women. It was the only time many of them saw silk.

Even bearing in mind that luxury magazines at this time were aiming at a fraction of the country's female population – and not even necessarily the most serious fraction at that – it all has an air of make-believe, of playing at being chic in wartime, and it is a relief to read in the same issue that 'the proudest women are those entitled to wear on their lapel the regimental badge of a husband, brother or beau' although unreality soon creeps back: 'Asprey makes them exquisitely in enamel, diamonds, rubies and sapphires...the smartest are the insignia of the Royal Navy, the Royal Air Force, Life Guards, the Royal Artillery, the Coldstream and Grenadier Guards.'

All of this did nothing to foreshadow the bravery and adaptability which women would show in

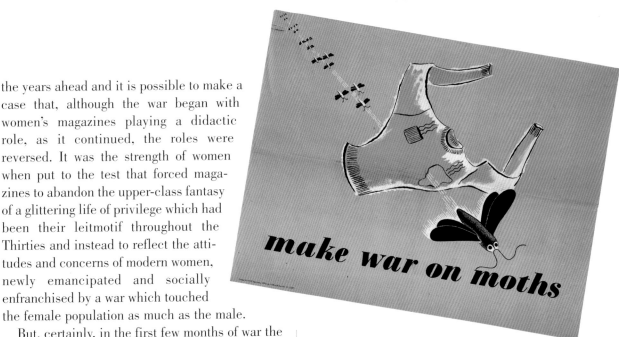

the years ahead and it is possible to make a case that, although the war began with women's magazines playing a didactic role, as it continued, the roles were reversed. It was the strength of women when put to the test that forced magazines to abandon the upper-class fantasy of a glittering life of privilege which had been their leitmotif throughout the Thirties and instead to reflect the attitudes and concerns of modern women, newly emancipated and socially enfranchised by a war which touched the female population as much as the male.

But, certainly, in the first few months of war the 'glossies' saw women in the passive role of support for their men. This was at variance with how the government was already seeing them. Knowing that the war effort would demand an active commitment from all fit and able-bodied citizens, regardless of their sex, it was keen to indoctrinate women with the knowledge that their role – in or out of uniform; in factories, on the land or merely 'keeping the home fires burning' – would be crucial. But its deep concern was maintaining the morale of the fighting men. The last thing government officials wanted was for female sex appeal to be subsumed by the masculine jobs they could increasingly be expected to do as the war effort dug deep.

In this, the government's great allies were the editors of women's magazines, and none more so than *Vogue* and *Harper's Bazaar*, for the huge authority they wielded, and *Good Housekeeping* for the practical, common-sense attitude for which it had always been known. All co-operated with the government to a degree which could be called propaganda, if not brain-washing, in a determined effort to enrol the hearts and minds of readers.

The change in editorial attitude was swift. In September 1939, *Harper's Bazaar* was still talking pure fashion-speak: 'The talk of the town is the new waist line,' its Paris report began, continuing with excited yelps of joy over 'the feathered toques and muffs, fantastic jewelled necklaces and tassels that might have come from the treasure of a Maharajah, and divine little bootees.' By January 1941, its leader page was given over to Harcourt Johnson, Minister in Charge, Department of Overseas Trade, making a bid for the support of women in the export drive. He ended on a stirring note which, it was hoped, would reconcile the women of Britain to the way in which austerity was already biting into all aspects of their lives, not least their appearance. He pointed out that, with the collapse of Paris and Vienna fashion centres, there was a 'gap that the United Kingdom textile industries have been quick to appreciate: every effort is being put forward to create a centre of women's fashions in Great Britain comparable with the pre-eminent position of London in the world of men's wear.' Everything, his message made clear,

As clothes supplies dwindled, the need to care for what you had became a priority.

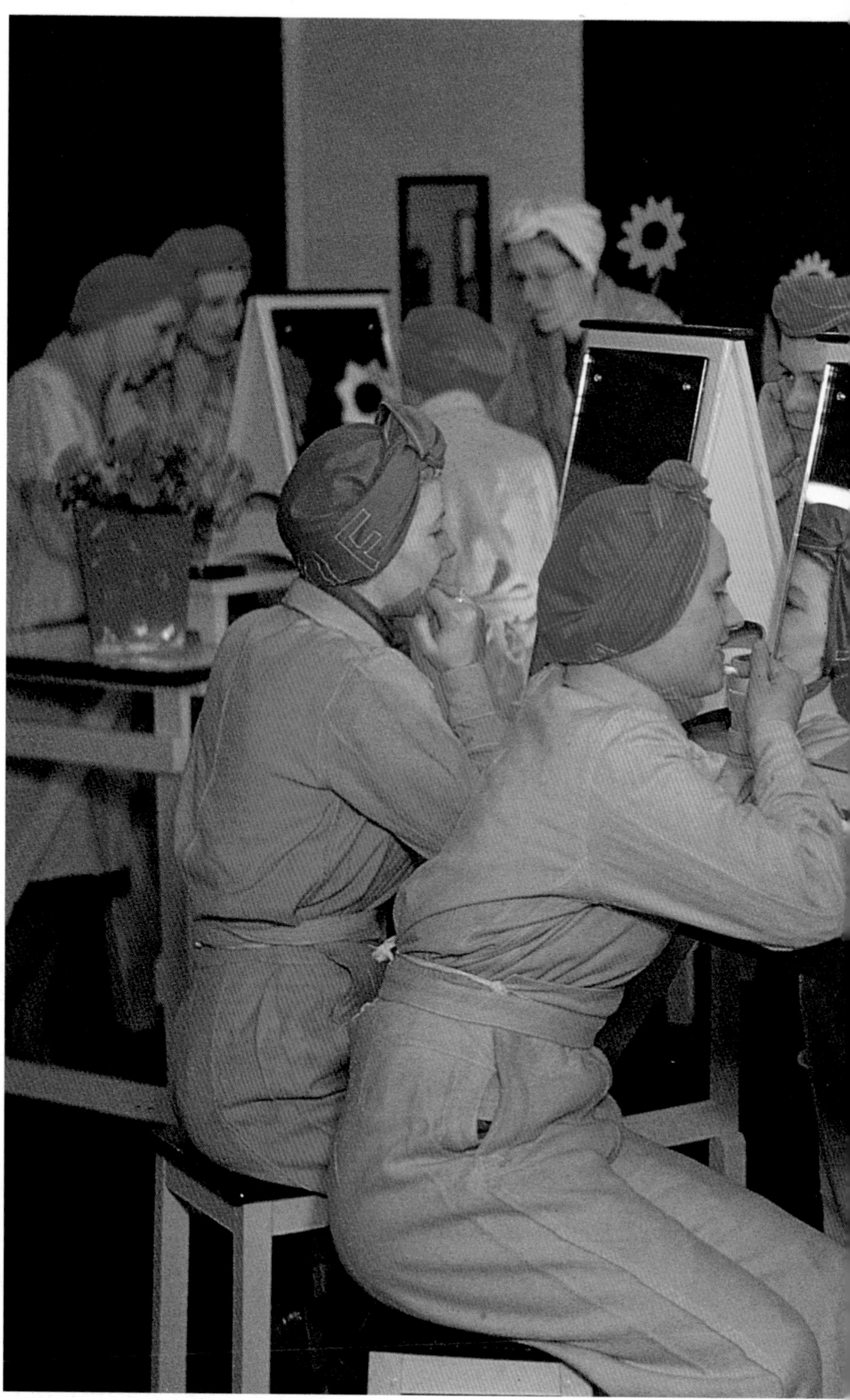

Done out like a beauty parlour, this make-up station at a Royal Ordnance factory was about safety rather than vanity. Munitions workers had to apply protective creams to prevent their skins absorbing toxic explosive powders.

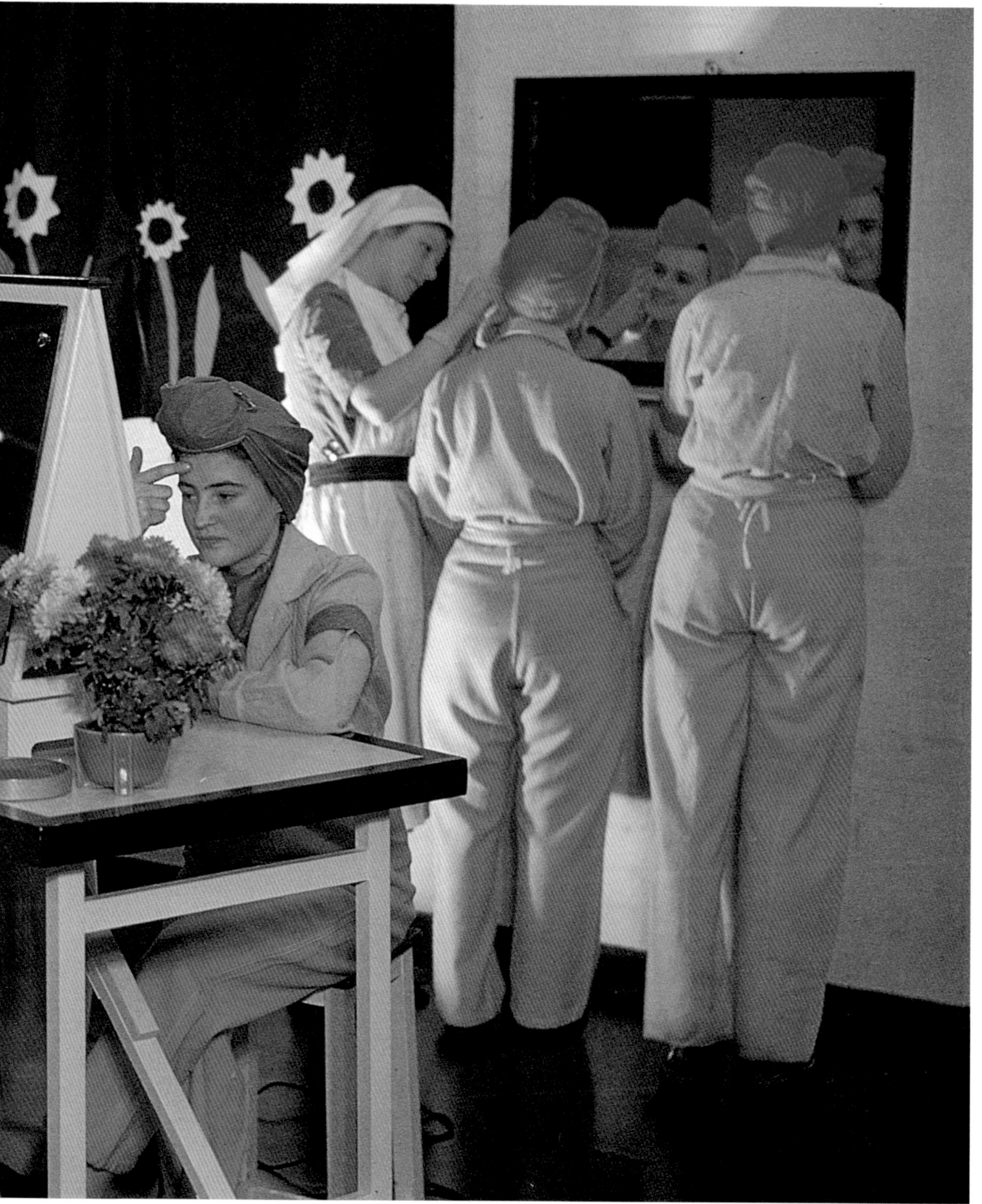

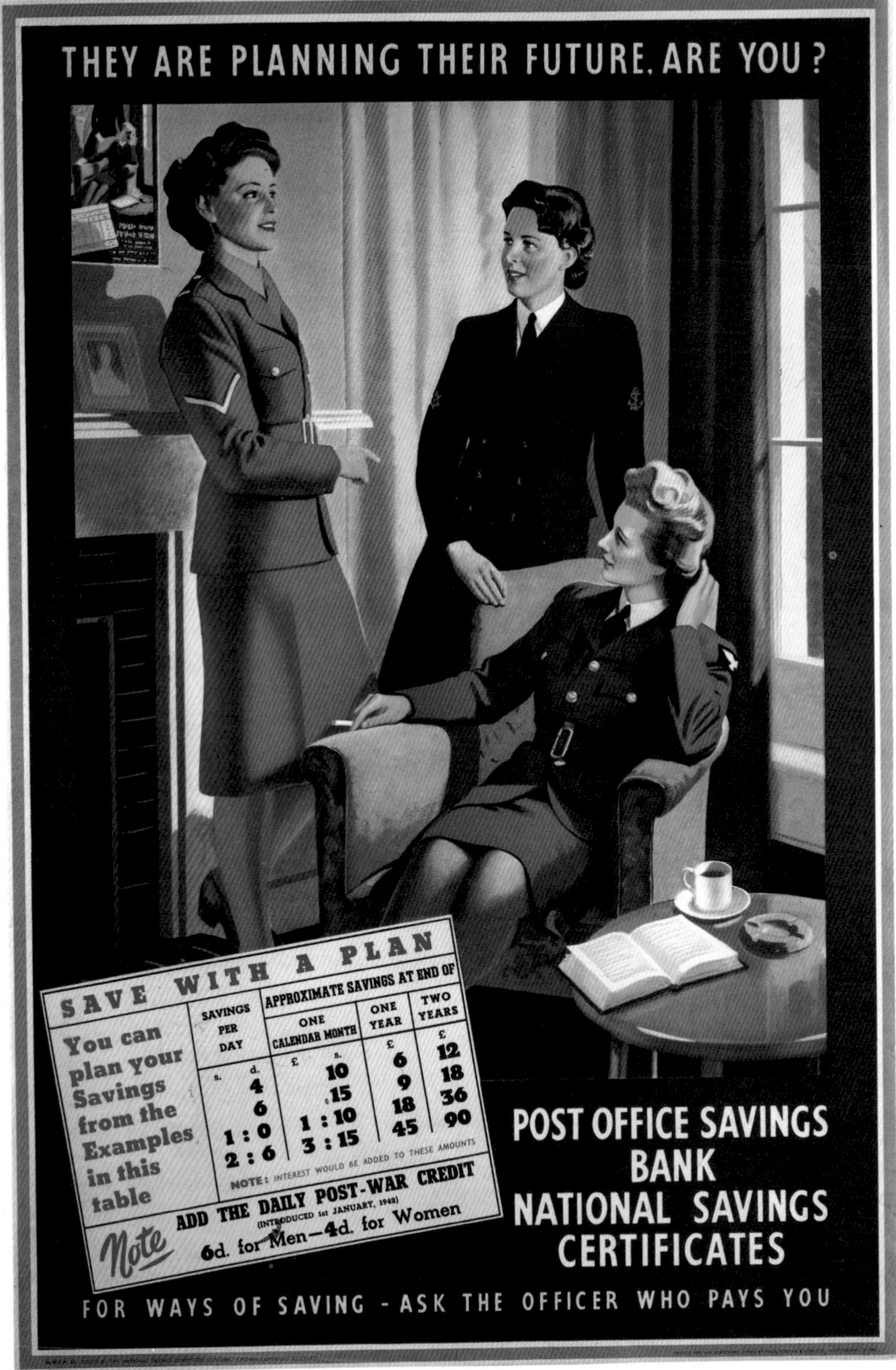
THEY ARE PLANNING THEIR FUTURE, ARE YOU?
SAVE WITH A PLAN
You can plan your Savings from the Examples in this table
SAVINGS PER DAY
APPROXIMATE SAVINGS AT END OF
ONE CALENDAR MONTH
ONE YEAR
TWO YEARS
s. d. | £ s. | £ | £
4 | 10 | 6 | 12
6 | 15 | 9 | 18
1 : 0 | 1 : 10 | 18 | 36
2 : 6 | 3 : 15 | 45 | 90
NOTE: INTEREST WOULD BE ADDED TO THESE AMOUNTS
Note
ADD THE DAILY POST-WAR CREDIT
(INTRODUCED 1st JANUARY, 1942)
6d. for Men—4d. for Women
POST OFFICE SAVINGS BANK
NATIONAL SAVINGS CERTIFICATES
FOR WAYS OF SAVING - ASK THE OFFICER WHO PAYS YOU

was now to be geared to the export drive.

What had happened in the intervening eighteen months? National Service for all fit adult males, Dunkirk and the Blitz were all to have great effects on women and the tenor of society which was reflected in their dress, but the biggest thing of all for fashion was the fall of France on 17 June 1940. The world fashion significance of this event is discussed in Chapter Four, but its instant effect was to stimulate British fashion to try to take over its role and, paradoxically, to make women realise that, instead of the supply of garments increasing, it was likely to shrink even further. It was the job of the 'glossies' to present this unpalatable fact in an upbeat way which would make it not only acceptable but even welcome. They did this by placing women at the psychological centre of the war effort.

As early as April 1940, under the heading 'The Return of the Soldier', *Vogue* was urging, 'Now, if ever, buy with crystal-clear conscience the clothes that will charm him.' This, of course, was before rationing, which was opposed by Churchill as being likely to affect morale, although government ministers were already examining the possibility of introducing a scheme for a standardised approach to clothing. There was even some talk that civilians should have a form of uniform – possibly based on the siren suit which Churchill found so convenient. As an idea it was stillborn. Not only would it have meant that people – mainly women, as female conscription had not yet begun – would be forced to abandon their perfectly serviceable existing clothes to the rigours of time and moth, it would have made the country's streets so dismal and drab that the effect on morale would have been disastrous.

On Reflection...
JOIN THE WAAF

LEFT: Service morale was kept high by encouraging the conviction that there was a civilian future worth planning for, when women would be in dresses again.

But, even though clothes and textile rationing were not imposed until June 1941, the glossies were writing enthusiastically of 'stay at home evenings', for which they suggested long woollen dresses for 'We must have warmth. There is nothing so plain as a blue nose.' *Vogue*'s shophound columnist wrote in the early months of the war, 'Nothing gives a feeling of *oomph* so much as having bespoke gloves' and proudly proclaimed that she had found them in doeskin at 7s 6d and capeskin for 8s 6d. So much for the realities of war – such prices were beyond the pockets of 80 per cent of women. However, for those who could afford them they would prove a boon: as fuel shortages bit and the fight against cold became serious, good gloves – which disappeared from the market with the leather shortage which was one of the characteristics of the war – were worth much more than their weight in gold.

Whilst the editorial staffs of *Vogue* and *Harper's Bazaar* were undergoing a spot of realism training in order to approach the new situation in a way that would have some meaning for their readers, *Good Housekeeping* was already taking a practical, no-nonsense approach which fitted perfectly with the publicity campaigns being cooked up by the Ministry of Information, the majority of which were aimed at women as the homemakers, feeders, clothers and, increasingly, breadwinners of civilian life. Even in the Thirties, it had carried features on fashion for the fuller figure and where the glossies talked of servants *Good Housekeeping* carried articles on down-to-earth characters such as charladies, a breed given a spirited defence in its pages by the popular novelist Frank Swinnerton.

But even *Good Housekeeping* was not immune from the obsession with woman as lady which had fascinated everybody in the Thirties and was still an iconic ideal in the Forties. A lady, according to the magazine, likes rouge on her cheeks – 'just enough to give a beguiling blush' – but does not like 'that just-out-of-the-dryer look' of set, rigid curls and waves. She loves perfumes with character – 'not too sweet, but crisp and rather dry' – but is wary of too much jewellery, especially 'piling it on so that it looks cluttery'. Without a doubt, the staff at *Good Housekeeping* would have entirely endorsed the early wartime advertisements for Boot's beauty preparations which claimed that there was 'still time for charm' and pointed out 'uniforms, yes, but not uniformity. The girl in service kit preserves her own personality, her own charm.'

Because it had such a broad appeal and reached a wide range of women, *Good Housekeeping* was chosen by the government for its advertisements extolling the efforts required of women during the war. 'Jack's in the Navy, serving our ships at sea; Jill's in the post office, saving her money to help him,' the National Savings Committee told readers. 'Joan's doing a *real* job. That's what I like about her. She's not playing at war work. Once she heard my story of what women *could* do for our chaps she was off like a flash to

The Land Army was one of the toughest of war jobs. Girls employed on farms had to be equipped to face all weathers and work in very uncomfortable conditions.

Recruiting posters for the Land Army featured pristine clothing and shining shoes rarely found at farm level.

NATIONAL SERVICE
WOMEN'S
LAND ARMY
SEASONAL LAND WORKERS
ENROL TODAY
FOR PARTICULARS apply to MINISTRY OF AGRICULTURE & FISHERIES (Women's Land Army) WHITEHALL PLACE, LONDON, S.W.1.

The smartest headgear for women was the forage cap, used on posters but not always issued to all ranks.

join the WAAF,' the Air Ministry ad proclaimed, whilst under the heading of 'No Surrender' a Yardley advertisement caught the same spirit: 'War gives us a chance to show our mettle. We wanted equal rights with men; they took us at our word. We are proud to work for victory beside them... We must achieve masculine efficiency without hardness... Never must we consider careful grooming a quisling gesture...'

What *Good Housekeeping* and its advertisers were doing was acknowledging a fact: the war had turned society on its head and, although it had refreshed and renewed many moribund corners of British life, there was a perceived danger that women might become so modern and masculine in their new-found freedom that they would turn their backs on their feminine and maternal instincts. Many thought that, despite the privations, young women – in thousands of cases released for the first time from family and community control, drafted as civilians and servicewomen to different parts of the country, even the world – were having too much fun. 'It's being so cheerful as keeps me going': Mona Lot's catchphrase on the wireless made people laugh, but there was a lurking suspicion that after the war women would not be the same again, even if their bathrooms and kitchens were stuffed with the things which had disappeared from the shops since 1939.

Certainly, the war was an eye-opening and liberating experience for millions of women. Becoming a Land Girl, for instance, gave many women from poor backgrounds a wardrobe – that is a *range* of different kinds of dress – for the first time. Standard 'issue' was generous: a hat, three shirts, one pullover, two pairs of breeches, two pairs of dungarees, two overall coats, six pairs of stockings, two pairs of slipper socks, one pair each of leather shoes and boots, leggings, gumboots, an oilskin or mackintosh and an overcoat.

Not only were many women comfortably dressed against the weather for the first time; even more became physically fit for the first time also. In the ATS, the accepted but unofficial approach was to wait at least a week before issuing new recruits with a complete uniform, because the physical exercise involved in drill and gym work tended to slim down the overweight, whilst the nutritionally regular food plumped out the skinny and underfed.

And standards were raised in other ways. Women who had never thought to look after their teeth did so now. Before conscription many women from poor backgrounds had never seen a sanitary towel and were still using the age-old method of rags which were soaked in cold, salted water ready for the next month.

In some respects, the women in uniform had a better war than those left in civilian life. At least they were clothed and fed without any effort on their part. Initially, the forces' requirement for women was judged to be small and the appeal of uniform attracted two distinct social classes. The middle-class girl, often from an 'officer class' background, joined up in a hearty – even debbie – spirit of derring-do. The girl who took her orders, from the poorer classes, was quick to enlist because she saw an opportunity to escape a narrow and empty social life. But things changed in December 1941 with the National Service (No. 2) Act, which made unmarried women and widows without children liable for military service, up to the age of 30 – although, in fact, conscription was limited to women between 18 and 25. By March 1942 *Harper's Bazaar* was putting a gloss on a necessity. 'It's the fashion,' an editorial claimed, 'to wear service uniform if you

The WVS in uniform designed by Digby Morton, supervising the National Emergency Washing Services, sponsored by Unilever, to overcome the effects of air raids and shortages of soap.

American uniforms were generally considered smarter than those issued in Britain. Certainly their material and cut were superior.

can, whether it's the ATS, the WRNS, the WAAF, the Red Cross or the WVS – you who wear it are the fashionables of today,' adding a cheery postscript: 'Be as carefree on leave as you are efficient on duty.'

Nevertheless, female conscription was revolutionary. Never before had women in Britain been called up and, initially at least, the War Office seems to have been at a loss how to deal with them. Discipline was an immediate problem. Traditionally ruthlessly brutalising, service life hardened up men who in most cases had to be tough enough to kill, but such approaches were clearly inappropriate for women. A solution was found through class, the vade-mecum of British social life. In a Thirties country house Upstairs Downstairs scenario, the other ranks were treated by the officers rather as domestic servants were treated by the mistress of the house. In a hierarchy which echoed that below stairs, housekeeper and cook transformed into NCOs helped to control women by making them feel they were 'in service' to the nation. The officer was the mistress, who even had to be called ma'am, the other ranks the housemaids, scullery girls and bottle washers to those upstairs.

It was a ruse what worked, buoyed up on a wave of patriotic euphoria which made women proud to play a part in the ultimate man's world and wear the uniform, even though many were condemned to jobs of domestic drudgery. There is nothing more masculine than the life of the soldiery, who are trained to act valiantly and are rewarded with decorations when they do so. It is significant of how the government expected the role of women to develop that the National Service (No. 2) Act made women in uniform also eligible for such honours, including the Victoria Cross. But tradition dies hard and most conscripted women were employed in uniform to carry out age-old female roles they had played out of it: cooking and domestic; secretarial and clerical; with some being involved in technical and mechanical roles. And there were pecking orders. The WRNS was by far the most popular service, not only because its members worked with naval officers, but also because they wore what was generally considered the smartest kit. This official dress issue consisted of two uniforms, flattering and chic in navy; a well-tailored navy greatcoat, some of which were made by Hector Powe although the majority came from Burtons; three white shirts; a gaberdine mac; two pairs of shoes; three pairs of directoire knickers in navy – commonly known as 'black-outs' – and a duffle coat for specific jobs of work. A great cause of irritation for women in the WAAF was that WRNS were given coupons for stockings and they were not. To compound the sense of wrong, *their* issue stockings were thick lisle. Although Digby

Women in ARP uniforms from Lillywhite playing gin rummy, which *Vogue* called the 'perfect card game' for wartime as it required no partner.

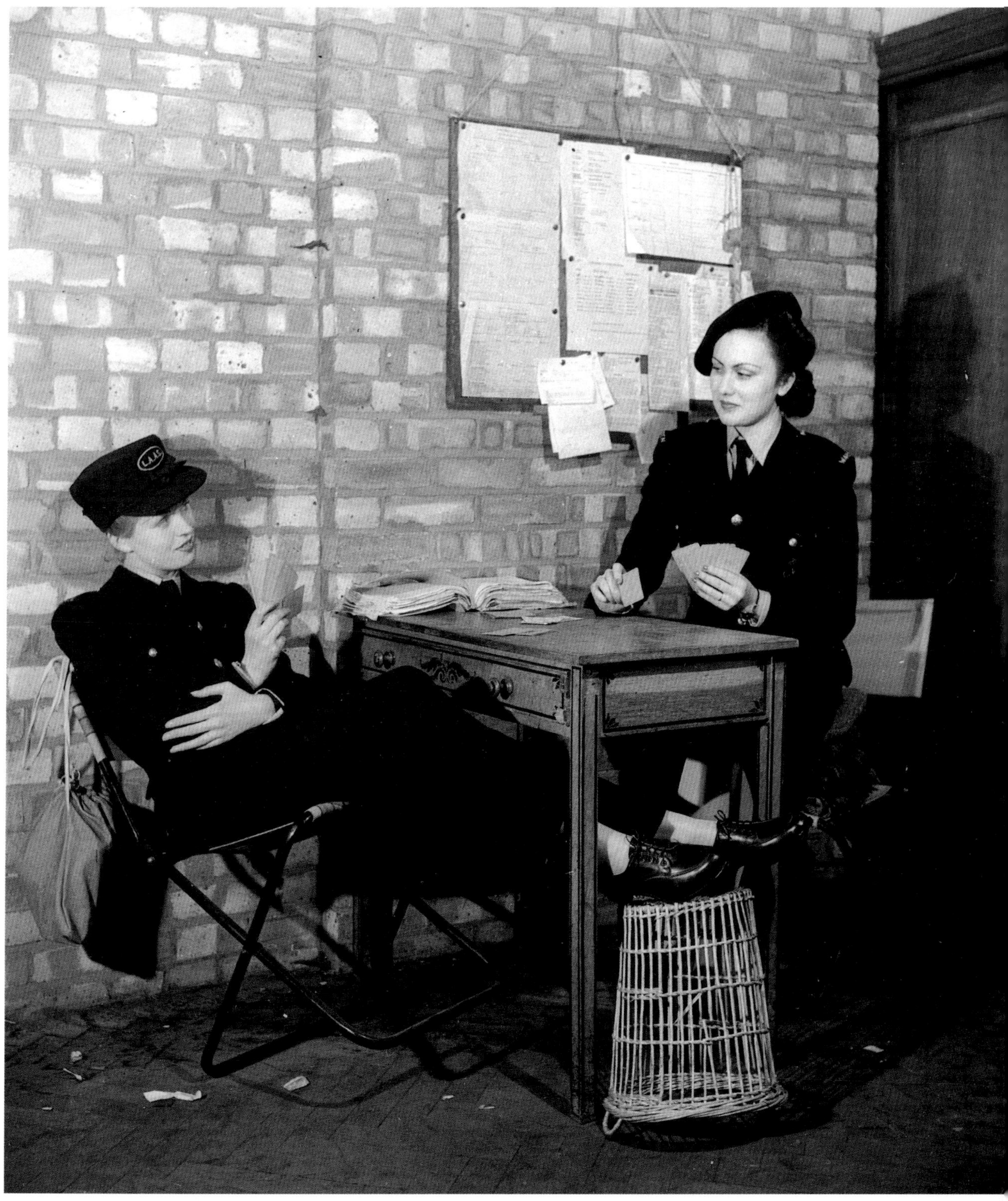

Morton designed the WVS uniform and Hartnell was consulted about the post-war relief work uniform of the Girl Guides, it was alien to British government thinking to link fashion and uniform in the way that other countries did: in Paris, the Benedict Bureau Unit, a nursing auxiliary group, wore a uniform designed by Molyneux, consisting of a navy blue dress with the letter BBU picked out on the collar, a navy blue overcoat and a cap.

Mass manufacturers supported the coupon scheme, despite the restrictions it placed on their output.

Unlike US nurses, whose cap and 'no-iron' seersucker overseas uniform were designed in consultation with Dorothy Shaver, prestigious design co-ordinator for the Fifth Avenue fashion store Lord & Taylor, or the WAVES, whose uniform was designed by Mainbocher, creator of the Duchess of Windsor's wedding dress – he gave them a white-capped hat which was considered the acme of chic, as were his uniforms for the US Red Cross and the Women Marines – British women in the forces were drably kitted out. Even so, desperately looking on the bright side, British *Vogue* pointed out in December 1941 that there was *some* choice in ATS uniform. Mentioning the fact that there was a wide variety of shades of khaki and types of material within regulations, the magazine suggested that ready-to-wear uniforms from Austin Reed, a man's tailor, were good value, as was Simpson of Piccadilly, who offered a forty-eight-hour – and, in extremely urgent cases, even a twenty-four-hour – service. For made-to-measure uniforms, Burberry and Lillywhites were considered the best.

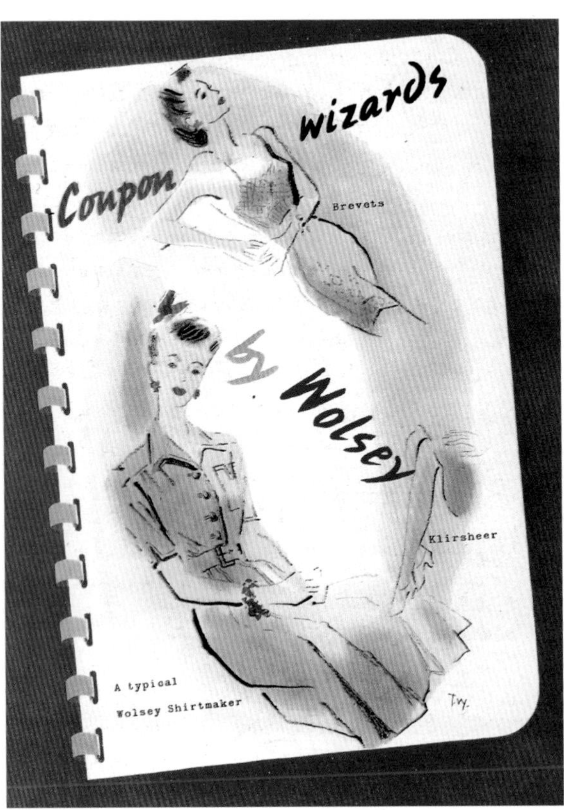

As when kitting out men, every item of clothing likely to be required was provided, including underwear. Army-issue bras and the notorious fleecy-lined knickers known as 'passion-killers' were a joke to the more sophisticated female recruits, many of whom would have preferred to be issued with coupons in order to exercise their own choice. But, having taken on responsibility for clothing service women, the government did it thoroughly, although with no thought of glamour or sex appeal. ATS recruits were lucky to get vests and knickers issued in cream wool. They were quite as likely to be given them in khaki.

Of course, whatever they were issued they were forced to rely on: with no coupons available their uniform frequently became their dress as much off duty as on. Whereas civilian women took pains to remake and modernise pre-war clothes, service women rarely had the time. If they went to a dance – especially on the camp – they tended to take the easy way out and wear uniform. It was an approach unofficially encouraged by authority because it

Princess Elizabeth in ATS uniform is watched by the Queen wearing her trademark pearls and exuberant hat.

was seen as a form of bonding in the 'we're all in this together' way which was so vital to wartime morale, while still exerting a measure of discipline.

Dress rules, enforced as strictly for women as for men, were normally relaxed to the extent that jackets could be removed for dancing, but ties had to be worn at all times, even when doing the Lambeth Walk or the Hokey-Cokey.

Leave presented problems for some service women. Whereas many wore their uniforms with pride, others desperately needed to be civilians again, if only briefly. And, although to modern eyes fashion changes during the war years seem slight, there were fads, often so local that service women knew nothing about them. A rare delivery of an item of dress – or, more likely, an accessory – long unobtainable was enough to make it an essential for every woman in the town. A woman returning for forty-eight hours' leave was disadvantaged not merely because she wasn't there to join the inevitable queue, but also because, if the item required coupons, she was ineligible to buy it in any case.

Service life – and the rules regulating it – was based on middle-class principles. The most important for women was the insistence on cleanliness, neatness and suitability of dress. It was especially appropriate that Lever Brothers used as one of their wartime advertising campaigns for Lifebuoy toilet soap (3½d for a 3 oz bar, plus one coupon) an information column concerning women in uniform which they called 'What They Do and What They Wear.' The advertisement featuring the ATS, for example, informed the public that 'The Director herself had a hand in the design of the smart, workmanlike ATS uniform' which was described as consisting of a 'simple cut square-shouldered tunic and slim-fitting skirt... Off duty they wear a smart field-service cap in chocolate or beech brown and leaf green.' And, of course, kept themselves spotlessly clean with Lifebuoy.

'Personal freshness' – one of the Lifebuoy obsessions – was of importance in and out of the services. Women shuddered and thought their lot not so bad when they read in the papers that in Paris, occupied by the Nazis, not only there was no coal to heat bath water but soap had virtually disappeared.

Adorable
loveliness
Fresh, radiant charm
True beauty comes with a lovely complexion and an air of exquisite freshness. That's where Lifebuoy Toilet Soap can help you! Its special ingredient makes it extra mild, a real safeguard for the complexion every time it's used. And in your bath that deep-cleansing lather brings a delightful feeling of renewed Personal Freshness.
LIFEBUOY TOILET SOAP
3½d tablet—1 coupon
LBT 616-925
LEVER BROTHERS, PORT SUNLIGHT, LIMITED

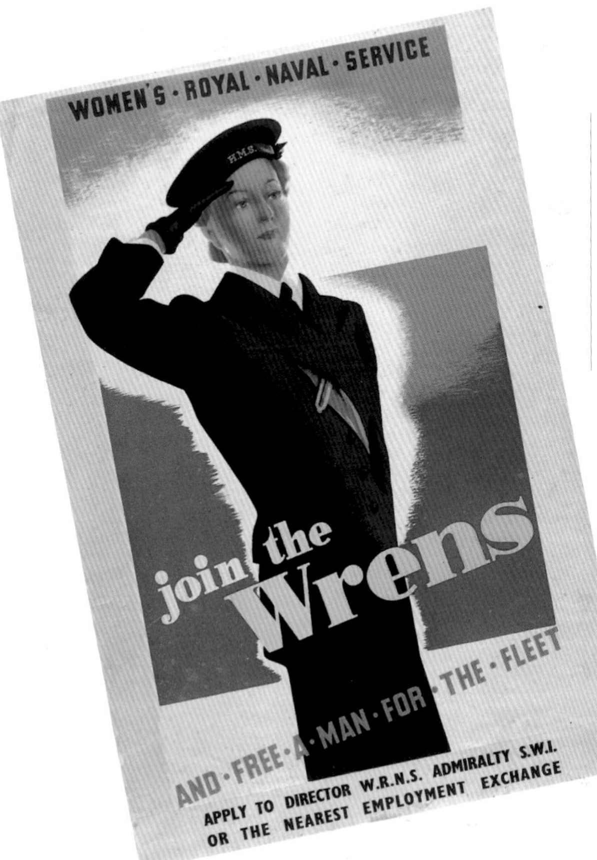

WOMEN'S · ROYAL · NAVAL · SERVICE
H.M.S.
join the Wrens
AND · FREE · A · MAN · FOR · THE · FLEET
APPLY TO DIRECTOR W.R.N.S. ADMIRALTY S.W.1.
OR THE NEAREST EMPLOYMENT EXCHANGE

The WRNS was the most popular of the women's forces, partly because its chic navy uniform flattered all figures.

Beauty products became increasingly scarce in Britain as all efforts and most raw materials were diverted into the war. No matter what the raw material, if it had any military use – in ammunition and armaments in particular – it virtually disappeared from civilian shop counters, although mysteriously appearing quite regularly beneath them.

Even when products were in such short supply as to be almost unobtainable, firms continued to advertise. It was considered valuable that they do so. No matter what privations they underwent, nobody wanted women to lose heart. It was recognised that for many, morale rested on a personal sense of femininity and glamour which must be maintained as far as possible. And so must hope. The advertisements for beauty, hair and make-up products were based on an illusion, but it was important that they be regularly published in newspapers and magazines even if they did, more often than not, contain an apology that the product would not be available until after the war. Bourjois, creators of 'Evening in Paris' – along with 'California Poppy', one of the most popular scents in the world in the late Thirties – produced advertisements called 'Bourjois and the Factory Front' in which women were told that they must wait for the perfume but could 'still enjoy the exquisite thrill of it' in their other beauty aids, including soap and hair preparations. Lux, 'the Beauty Soap of the Film Stars', suggested in its advertisements that buying its brand was a patriotic as well as practical gesture: 'You see, the lather made by Lux Toilet Soap is more abundant than the lather made by ordinary soaps.' So, you saved money *and* water by using it!

Beauty houses and government were keen to prove that, despite shortages, women could still look attractive, even in uniform.

What were the things about which women dreamed when manning fire posts, waiting to drive the generals, plotting the paths of fighter planes – or, more prosaically if not in uniform, potting baby, queuing for the meat ration or digging for victory? Pre-war glamour and the products exemplifying it, even though, in many cases, they had not been able to afford them in the Thirties. And it was the advertisements that kept the dream alive.

In a sense, women in the services found it more vital to hang onto the few vestiges of femininity permitted them. A world where they were put on a charge for trivial offences – such as not wearing the hat important for the salute seen as vital for

SEEING IT THROUGH

How proud upon your quarterdeck you stand,
Conductor – Captain – of the mighty bus!
Like some Columbus you survey the Strand,
A calm newcomer in a sea of fuss.

You may be tired – how cheerfully you clip,
Clip in the dark, with one eye on the street –
Two decks – one pair of legs – a rolling ship –
Much on your mind – and fat men on your feet!

The sirens blow, and death is in the air:
Still at her post the trusty Captain stands,
And counts her change, and scampers up the stair,
As brave a sailor as the King commands.

A. P. Herbert

remained of the Thirties: Kestos Bras – 'Woman has no surer ally'; Berlei foundation garments – 'takes inches off my figure and years off my age'; Barbara Gould Plastic Cream – '20 Minute Magic: 'lovely today, more lovely tomorrow' – may not have survived the war; Elbeo stockings also temporarily disappeared. But advertisements kept alive hope for women in the services and those guarding 'the home fires', ready for their return.

Many of these women were also in uniform, having taken over civilian jobs left empty by the draft. Their contribution to transport was especially important. The female 'clippie' soon became a feature on most bus routes, her uniform a quick adaptation of that worn by male bus conductors. Railway guards and station personnel were as likely to be women as men – and dressed in the same way. But it was the women who worked in factories whose 'uniform' has come down to us as the enduring image of the female contribution to the war effort. Expected to do remarkably heavy physical work, put in very long hours and master skills which had taken peacetime apprentices years rather than months to achieve, they were the true heroines of the period. Dressed in protective clothing, their appearance had none of the glamour of their service counterparts. And neither did their jobs. Many women suffered nervous breakdowns due to the pressure, especially of the constant din heard in most factories.

Overalls and dungarees were so depressingly utilitarian – and that, unfortunately, was how so much of fashion was going. It was all right to breathe a sigh of relief that the rigid class structure of Thirties fashion was finally breaking down but women had, for centuries, used their

Factories were noisy and dirty. Although not flattering, turbans kept hair clean and protected it from dangerous machinery.

THE SATURDAY EVENING
POST
Y 29, 1943
10¢
BEGINNING—A NEW
KELLAND SERIAL
Heart on Her Sleeve
EDGAR SNOW
REPORTS ON GERMAN
ATROCITIES
ROSIE
Norman
Rockwell
MEIN
KAMPF

Rosie the Riveter knew how essential her work in heavy industries was to the war effort and wore her dungarees with pride.

clothes to express themselves. What were they to do now? After the first careless rapture of wearing clothes long out of fashion, comfortable old shapes into which they could snuggle without any of the usual fandango – *and* know that they were being patriotic by being sloppy – the spirit reasserted itself and frustration and depression at the *sameness* of dress began to take over.

As the war effort bit deeper, most of the fashions shown in magazines were available only for export, if at all. For every woman encouraged by seeing pictures of beautiful clothes, even those she couldn't buy, there was at least one more who felt irritation at having her deprivations highlighted. In fact, if fashion can be defined as the thing done by the majority, then the most fashionable thing during the war years was to be unfashionable. Most women reduced their clothes buying to the minimum, as the government hoped they would. There was a tacit agreement that manufacturers and retailers were performing a holding operation, merely keeping things 'ticking over'.

The romantic elegance which was the daytime style of the late Thirties seemed far away and the evening looks, which carried women back on a wave of enthusiasm for the crinolines created by Hartnell for the Queen to the days of Winterhalter and the Empress Eugénie, were so inappropriate that they would have been swept away even if black-outs, fire-fighting and the Blitz had not put a total moratorium on such grand dressing. After all, they were an inept exercise in atavism even in the Thirties. By the early Forties, such clothes and the attitudes behind them were antediluvian.

But the classic backbone of English dressing was the tailor-made – the suit in soft wool tweed which London did better than anywhere else. That had reached a high point in the late Thirties. Influenced by Creed and Molyneux – British to their fingertips although, working in Paris, in no way parochial – the tweed costume was pared down and unfussy in a way which meant that even if it had not been such a psychological comfort (shades of continuity, of country values, of quality and class), it would survive as the practical basis of wartime fashion. As restrictions on material began to constrain designers, the suit became even more minimalist until it could actually be called severe.

Costume historians suggest that such severity was a form of solidarity with those in

Civilian life was increasingly influenced by the war, not least its fashions.

uniform, a deliberate echo of the sterility and practicality of service dress in which there was no place for decorative *joie d'esprit*. In fact, it was much more an economic decision, imposed more than inspired. There simply wasn't enough material for dresses to be as generously draped as they had been in the Thirties. Designers now had to try to provide a soft sophistication by shirring – not the same thing at all. For the same reason, the generous box pleats went and a mean little kick-pleat took their place. The archetypal wartime silhouette had little to do with ideology and everything to do with practicality. Small collars, narrow jackets and skirts, minuscule peplums, emphasis on seaming, draped bodices and narrow belts were all imposed by government restrictions.

That being said, the tailored look – found in dresses and coats as well as suits – did chime with the no-nonsense, efficiency-for-victory approach which dominated the thinking of the time. Women learned to live with a fashion that eschewed frivolity but still maintained a level of femininity – and to accept it without resentment.

One of the things they did resent, even while accepting its inevitability, was the fact that safety rules insisted that hair be covered when working with machinery. The actual covering was not a problem: even when there was no danger of hair being caught in machines, the atmosphere in many factories and workshops was so polluted that women were happy enough to cover their head to keep it clean. It was the unglamorous nature of the covering which upset many. The head scarf had none of the cachet of the forage cap of the services women. It was as dreary and unamenable to adaptation as the Thirties 'pinny' of the working-class housewife – and almost as ubiquitous. At a time when Veronica Lake's 'peekaboo' hairstyle, launched in 1943, glamorously cascading over one eye, was considered the last word in sexiness, it was hard for women to have to tuck every last strand under cover. Government-sponsored short hairstyles like the Victory Roll and the Liberty Cut had as much allure as a cold sausage roll by comparison. Even though, in response to a plea by the US Government, Veronica Lake changed her hair into an upswept style, the publicity it was given could not entirely eradicate the pull of the previous one.

The authorities tried to make covered heads a fashion statement in factories, but most women followed the edict reluctantly.

Long hair remained a staple of glamour throughout the war because, as rationing began to bite into every area of dress, hair became increasingly important as a means of maintaining one's morale, reassuring oneself of one's sexuality and having any pretence of keeping up with the fashion. The women who led the fashion were the film stars. Ann Todd, Margaret Lockwood and Celia Johnson were hugely popular. Their immaculate make-up, impeccable hairstyles and the perfect good taste of their costumes made them the

Veronica Lake's peekaboo hairstyle made hats seem very unsexy. Every woman wanted to look like her.

The reality of life without shampoo or setting lotion fell some way behind the Hollywood dream for those living at Home Guard level.

Celia Johnson in *Brief Encounter* wears a suit and hat as near to military cut as it is possible to get with tweed.

classic icons of English femininity. But there were other, more basic models who had considerably more appeal.

Hollywood's role in the war is well documented. The American government allowed production to continue almost without modification, although costume design was subject to the same restrictions imposed on clothes. It was accepted that a trip to the pictures was a major morale booster for millions, in and out of uniform. The government also knew that even the most popular and slick 'B' movie was solid propaganda for American values. Dorothy Lamour, Rita Hayworth, Hedy Lamarr and Lana Turner were certainly not as ladylike as their British equivalents, but they had considerably more oomph and sex appeal. The way they did their hair was noted by the women in the audience, who then did their best to get the same effect, using the limited means at their disposal. And limited they were. As the war continued, even hairpins became a luxury to be carefully hoarded; hairnet production was cut back dramatically and, as towels became in short supply and then laundry facilities disappeared, many hairdressers put up notices begging clients to bring their own towels.

Despite the difficulties, women rarely lost their spirit and most would have agreed with Yardley's stirring advertisement of 1942: 'We cannot leave men to fight this war alone. Total war makes heavy demands... The slightest hint of a drooping spirit yields a point to the enemy. Never must careless grooming reflect a "don't care" attitude...we must never forget that good looks and good morale are the closest of good companions. Put your best face forward.'

The women who read these words would have been perfectly justified in asking, 'Yes, but how?' In the year of Yardley's advertisement, the supply of beauty products fell to less than a quarter of the 1938 level. Major ingredients such as glycerin, castor oil, talc, fats, petroleum and alcohol were needed for the war effort. The factories which had manufactured cosmetics in peacetime, increasingly swung into producing items more directly linked to the needs of the war. At Cyclax, production was concentrated on sun barriers and cream to protect the skins of soldiers fighting in North Africa and at Yardley itself the workers were making more aircraft components and seawater purifiers than lipsticks.

Somehow, despite all

Ann Todd's chic hat had sombre undertones in 1945: the mourning veil was more than just a fashion statement.

restrictions, there always seemed to be some way of making up. Most expedients were considered not only wise but morally and socially sound. The Tangee advertisements, 'War, Women and Lipstick', put it in such a way that nobody could disagree: 'No lipstick – ours or anyone else's – will win the war. But it symbolises one of the reasons why we are fighting,' it claimed, ending by triumphantly proclaiming 'the precious right of women to be feminine and lovely under any circumstances.'

An ARP warden gives her make-up a final touch before going on duty.

Tales of makeshift cosmetics abound. The ends of used lipstick, which would once have been carelessly tossed out, were collected, melted together and poured into a container to resolidify. Not surprisingly – it has been calculated that many women had only two new lipsticks for the duration of the war. When lipstick ran out, solid rouge was used on lips. Soot and charcoal were used for eyeshadow. Rose petals steeped in water produced a liquid which gave a semblance of colour to cheeks. Even boot polish was used as an eyelid-darkener – until that, too, became scarce. To remove make-up, many women used a minute amount of lard rubbed into their faces, as cold creams and removal creams went off the market.

Actresses provided glamour in a world starved of it. Make-up and beauty houses employed the top Hollywood stars to endorse their products.

Talking to women who worked in factories or on the land during the war reveals a make-up pattern. For most of the week, it was not a great concern. 'Farms – and, indeed, factories – were no places for the fastidious female,' I was told by a rather grand woman who spent the war years in Northumberland. She recalled the destructive dirt which attacked the hands and complexions of her Land Girls. 'Threshing was a filthy job. Chaff got everywhere. In the winter, gathering turnips and sprouts – often stiff and hard with frost or snow-ruined hands. Nails broke; the quicks were cut; the knuckles bled. Chilblains were common. Some girls used to rub their hands with the salve used to soften cows' udders for milking, but I'm not sure it did any good.'

JOAN BENNETT *in Walter Wanger's* "HOUSE ACROSS THE BAY"

Your mirror will reveal a new complexion, when you try

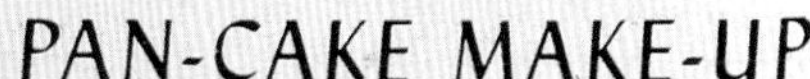

PAN-CAKE MAKE-UP

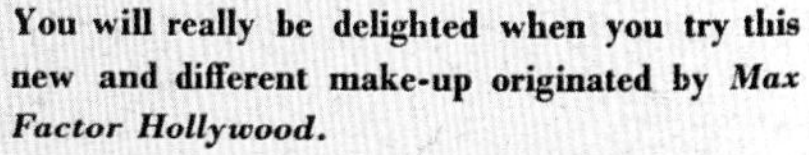

You will really be delighted when you try this new and different make-up originated by *Max Factor Hollywood.*

It imparts a smooth, velvety, youthful look!
It helps hide tiny complexion faults!
It stays on for hours without re-powdering!

First introduced in Technicolor pictures, Pan-Cake Make-Up is to-day's new make-up fashion.

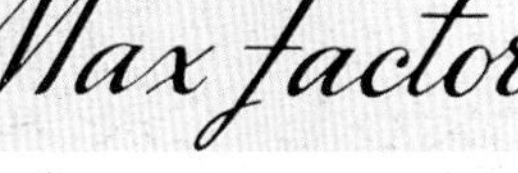

Rainbow Corner in London's West End was the place to show off a new hair-do to appreciative Yanks.

The highlight of the week, for the lucky ones, was the local hop – the unlucky ones had to wait a fortnight or even a month in remoter country areas. Then, appearance not only became important, it was uppermost in every girl's mind. Most dances were held on Friday or Saturday night and preparations began the night before, with a shampoo and set. If setting lotion wasn't available – and in many areas it disappeared from chemists' shelves for the duration of the war, although it could often be found with other priceless 'unobtainables' such as knicker elastic 'under the counter' at the local market if you knew which stall to go to – dampening the hair with sugar water before setting it was seen by many as a reasonable substitute.

In the lunch break, girls did each other's nails and discussed their make-up. Often, overtime and long shifts meant that work didn't finish until 8pm, so many changed at work, having brought their dress and shoes in a paper bag. The routine was as fast as it was efficient. Wash, take off head covering, curlers out, comb hair through. Then make-up, including a quick spit in the mascara box to moisten it, and finally dress. The last stage was to put on the precious pair of stockings and – if you had them – the high heels, although by 1943 they were limited to 2 inches and peep toes were entirely banned.

The dances were all very innocent, being more to do with fun and physically getting rid of the week's frustrations than sexual excitement. There was a naive, almost child-like heartiness about the Palais Glide and Lambeth Walk although, when the GIs arrived they brought the more athletic and sexually exciting boogie-woogie and jive. In fact, Rainbow Corner, the GI club created from a Lyons Corner House between Shaftesbury Avenue and Windmill Street, was not only renowned for the wildness of the dancing but notorious as a pick-up joint for sexual adventurers. But small towns and country districts, although not entirely free of sin, were less ostensibly raunchy. There the evening usually ended with the conga, the last waltz (the favourite tune being 'When I Grow Too Old to Dream'), the post horn gallop and maybe a final fling to 'American Patrol' – by which time what little make-up had been on faces to begin with had disappeared with exertion.

One of the major concerns of the cosmetic and beauty industries was how they might package even the reduced range of products they were allowed to offer the public. The raw materials of presentation – aluminium, bakelite, cellophane, cardboard and glass – were all deemed vital to the war effort. In Paris, women took their empty bottles back to Guerlain in order to have them refilled, as it was virtually impossible for the company to get its hands on new ones. In England, Yardley circumvented the problem by packaging many of its products in wax containers. It was not just the ingenuity of the commercially motivated.

It was the 'Dunkirk spirit' again, the refusal to be beaten by circumstances.

Much the same thinking was behind the most bizarre of all the examples of imagination in the face of shortages to have come from the war years. The idea of female modesty was one of the pre-war concepts which did not survive the war unmodified. Women accepted many things in the Forties which would have been unimaginable in the Thirties. But one of the things they found hardest to face was appearing in public without stockings. Older women in particular found it deeply embarrassing. They felt coarse, common, even vulnerable without them. One woman said she feared men would think she was 'available' when they saw her bare legs. As the difficulty in finding stockings became greater – even on the black market – women tried to find ways of disguising the bare-flesh look which made them feel so naked when exposing skin on something as intimate as their legs.

Tea dances, like this one at Grosvenor House, London, provided a much-needed opportunity to dress up and have a bit of fun.

Cosmetic companies, realising the problem, produced lotions which, like the leg make-up first introduced in the Twenties to simulate a South of France tan, could be painted on the skin to give a reasonably reliable and permanent covering. Cyclax called theirs – with admirable directness – Stockingless Cream and Elizabeth Arden's more sophisticated Fin 200 was claimed to be the perfect stocking substitute, able to resist rain, mud

NO MORE
LADDERS
We paint
your Stockings
on your legs

C H A P T E R 3

Life Goes On

Left: The ration book, an essential of the times. Above: Utility dresses, May 1942.

The imposition of clothes rationing was not popular with the government. The result was that, although food rationing came into force almost immediately after the declaration of war, the decision over clothes rationing was shelved until the demands of the war effort made it impossible to continue without it. Even so, it came much too late in one respect. By the time it was announced, on 1 June 1941 – a year and a half after food rationing – shortages and, more importantly at this stage, scares over shortages, had pushed up the price of clothes in a way in which the government had not allowed to happen with food. So, the scheme started under a cloud. Unlike food rationing, which had taken everyone by surprise, clothes rationing had been on the cards long enough for the richer echelons of society to buy up what they might need, the poorer to organise themselves to a certain degree and the black marketeers to get themselves ready for what they hoped would be a killing.

Few expected rationing to last long. Nobody could have imagined the degree of shortage which the country would face not just during but also after the war. If it could have been foreseen, would the reaction to rationing have been as positive as it was?

With the Utility scheme, the number of coupons required became as pressing as the price in choosing what to buy.

The British have a concept of fair play

4 IN "WOOL" AT ONLY 2 COUPONS A YARD!
Cunningly woven to look like wool this new Utility rayon fabric costs just 2 coupons and 5s. 2d. a yard— it's new and it's news. You'll find it in Selfridge's and most of the other big stores
Pattern No. 4257 has a neat, buttoned coat-front. In bust sizes 32 to 40; size 34 takes 3¾ yd. of 36-in. material. Price 1s. 3d., post free, from the address on page 53.
14
Pattern No. 3981 with four trim pockets is in bust sizes 32 to 38; size 34 takes 4¾ yd. of 36-in. material. Price 1s. 3d., post free, om the address on page 53.
Pattern No. 4294 has raglan-style sleeves and a wide skirt. In bust sizes 32 to 38; size 34 takes 3¾ yd. of 36-in. material. Price 1s. 3d., post free, from the address on page 53.
Pattern No. 3999 has that elegantly simple look. It is in bust sizes 32 to 38; size 34 takes 3¾ yd. of 36-in. material. Price 1s. 6d., post free, from the address on page 53.
15

Wool and angora makes Wolsey's rose-beige (new autumn pastel) afternoon dress, with a fall-in-front bodice. Harrods
Royal blue—bright change from black—for Wolsey's shirt dress of angora and wool with little-girl gathered pockets. Harrods
Petrol blues for Laura Lee's tailored plaid dress of Tested-Quality
fabric made with Courtaulds rayon. Galeries Lafayette

Francis Marshall managed to make even austerity fashions look chic, although the reality was often a different story.

considered exaggerated by many foreigners, who tend to take a more robust approach to emergencies by frequently allowing them to find their own level. In Italy, for example, there was no rationing during the war. In England, the government was determined to see fair shares for all. In practice, this meant basic entitlement for all, with a little discreet leeway for those with more money and social power than the rest. Nevertheless, the scheme lived up to the government's ideals which were to ensure that sufficient clothes were available and affordable and that the civilian population was properly clad; to see that materials were used to maximum effect and, not least, to keep the nation's morale – especially that of the female population – high. Even the most benighted member of the Cabinet recognised that the British belief in the importance of 'keeping up appearances' must be upheld in a way that benefited as many as possible and, as far as was realisable in such a class-conscious society, across as many social barriers as it could.

As early as March 1941, the gaps were showing. The general cost of living was up by 29 per cent on 1939 but clothes had shot up by 69 per cent. The main reason was purchase tax, introduced in October 1940. Most garments and footwear attracted tax at 16 per cent but furs, silk, gloves, head shawls, hairnets, veils, belts, suspenders, shoe laces, corset laces, hair and curling pins all paid 33 per cent. The government knew that the cost of clothing must be stabilised in the fairest way possible and concluded that a rationing policy affecting everybody was the best way to do it. The decision seemed to the public to have been made in great haste. At the time of the announcement, clothing coupons had not even been printed and people used their margarine coupons for clothes.

The President of the Board of Trade, Oliver Lyttleton, whose responsibility rationing was, tried to sweeten what he knew would be for many a bitter pill. 'When you are tired of your old clothes,' he urged, 'remember that by making them do you are contributing some part of an aeroplane, a gun or a tank.' The concept was developed by the Board of Trade into the 'Make Do and Mend' campaign which was to become a bedrock of the country's fight against waste. While women worried about how they would cope with clothing children who outgrew or wore out their clothes at an alarming pace, the sleek were not unduly fazed. As the Tory MP 'Chips' Channon wrote in his diary, sixty-

Go through your wardrobe
Make-do and Mend
BOARD OF TRADE

It became every woman's patriotic duty to 'Make Do and Mend', as government propaganda never failed to point out.

six coupons per year (which was everybody's entitlement) was not generous, especially as a man's suit took twenty-six, before adding, 'Luckily, I have 40 or more [suits]... I have enough clothes to last me for years.' This sort of social unbalance was not likely to be evened up by any rationing policy. The rich were simply too far ahead for anyone to catch them.

To help people through what many saw as the jungle of clothing regulations the Board of Trade issued a small booklet called 'Clothing Coupon Quiz' which set out to give 'Answers to Questions on the Rationing of Clothing, Footwear, cloth and Knitting Yarn'. It cost 2d. Its introduction had distinctly schoolmasterly tones. 'There is enough for all if we share and share alike,' it began. 'Rationing is the way to get fair shares. *Fair shares* – when workers are producing guns, aeroplanes and bombs instead of frocks, suits and shoes. *Fair shares* – when ships must run the gauntlet with munitions and food rather than with wool and cotton. *Fair shares* – when movements of population outrun local supplies. It is your scheme – to defend you as a consumer and as a citizen. All honest people realise that trying to beat the ration is the same as trying to cheat the nation.'

This was followed by an explanation of how the scheme would work and a comprehensive table detailing the number of coupons required for the principal articles of adults' and children's clothing. Already aware of the fact that the demand for pure wool was unlikely to be met, the table pointed out that '"woollen" in relation to any rationed goods means more than 15 per cent by weight of wool' and added that 'fur' included imitation fur. Coupon-free articles included headgear other than that made from scarves or 'incorporating handkerchiefs', which meant that millinery would continue untrammelled. Was this a deliberate psychological sop to keep up female morale? Certainly, at this stage, her hat was one of the most important considerations in a woman's outfit and the news that they were not to be rationed must have cheered many women already wondering how they would cope with the restrictions.

To cut out the element of wondering as far as possible, the second part of the booklet consisted of a question and answer section which covered, in great detail, most eventualities – from how men in the service would obtain clothing to the regulations concerning the clothing and footwear for prisoners of war. The reader discovered that coupons were required for domestic servants' uniforms; how district nurses were to obtain their uniforms; and that an extra allowance of fifty clothing coupons was available to expectant mothers. Most bizarrely the government had no objection to anyone purchasing a single shoe, sock or glove, 'if the shopkeeper doesn't object'. In theory, interchange of coupons was allowed only between people in the same family but, almost immediately, the poor began to sell their coupons to the better off – the beginning of a black-market ruse which flourished throughout the war.

Another loophole was the ruling that second-hand articles of clothing, if 'genuine', were exempt from coupons. This was an acknowledgment by the government that many of the working classes bought their staple items of dress at jumble sales and market stalls but, in fact, the ruling misfired, making the local market a Mecca for 'spivs' and a clearing house for black-market goods, including items looted from bombed shops, warehouses and even homes. The government did not stretch the leeway given to second-hand goods to cover the other source of working clothing, the Clothing Clubs, where items were bought on 'the never-never,' so called, cynics claimed, because the buyer never owned the clothing as it was worn out before it was paid for, at 2d per week to the tallyman who called at the door. The ruling was that coupons had to be handed to the supplier before the goods were supplied. Payment was on the 'never-never', but coupons were not.

A hat and belt made from pre-war scraps of material, 'now coupons are scarce'.

Considerable ingenuity was employed to ensure that odd pieces of material could still create something 'presentable'.

An almost immediate effect of the announcement of clothes rationing was the volte face performed by the glossy magazines. No more reports like that of Lady Mendl's famous circus ball at Versailles in 1939 – already seeming as if it had taken place on another planet – with its troop of white horses 'brought specially from Finland'. Inspired by the government's determination, editors were now preoccupied by the practicalities. And they were perfectly sincere in their monthly

EMERGENCY FASHION
GREAT AIR FORCE
Schiaparelli designs a LITTLE DRESS for these times
IN VIYELLA THIRTY-SIX FASHION FABRICS
Here is Schiaparelli meeting today's fashion need: a dress you can live in and stay smart in— wash one day and wear the next.
She chose a check Viyella Thirty-six in Autumn's own colours, brown, yellow and a bright berry red.
Viyella Thirty six—Plain shades and marls, blouse checks and stripes, 4/11 a yard. Lovely dress designs in novel woven effects, 5/11 a yard. All 36" wide.
All prices now subject to War Emergency increases.
WILLIAM HOLLINS AND COMPANY LIMITED · VIYELLA HOUSE · NOTTINGHAM · ENGLAND

Top designers were called in to create dresses which looked smart without breaking the restrictions codes.

exhortations to women. They knew the difficulties faced by all but the most privileged of their sex and they did not need the government to instruct them to emphasise the importance of the female role. Their object was simple enough – to hit the precise note which would make accepting the new restrictions not merely a duty but also a pleasure, giving a sense of pride and patriotism as women rose above the difficulties and, in an often used headline, carried on with 'Business as Usual'.

Optimism was the key word. It had started early on. In January 1941 *Vogue* greeted the ban on silk stockings positively. The available substitutes – in rayon or cotton – were praised as 'both marvellously like silk'. Whether such euphoria fooled women is arguable, but it surely helped them face life with fortitude. And things, as yet, were not too bad. In autumn 1941, a woman could buy a wool crepe dress 'to wear for tea on a winter afternoon' from Harrods for 69s 6d and eleven coupons. A rayon shirt dress by Rembrandt could be had from Galeries Lafayette for 5 guineas and seven coupons; a herringbone tweed coat by the fashionable ready-to-wear tailor H. J. Nicholl, 'in a large range of colours', for 8 guineas and eighteen coupons.

Fashion marched on. In November 1941 *Women's Wear Daily*, the American fashion trade newspaper, commented, 'A forecast that, when women could only buy a very few clothes, they would buy from better houses has worked out; most of the dressmakers have names on their books which are new since June 1st, the date when rationing commenced.' The rich and fashionable were looking ahead and investing in quality. Nevertheless, those fashion houses which were still functioning were taking no chances. They increasingly concentrated on renovating and remaking – even restyling – the clothes of their established customers, knowing that many of the new women were backed by 'easy-come, easy-go' money from black-market speculations and racketeering. In any case, reworking old clothes required no coupons, so it was a trade that could be expected to continue for the duration. An article in *Harper's*

There were times when it all became too much and women protested against the difficulties, even though they knew nothing could be done.

Berkertex Utility clothes, designed under Norman Hartnell's supervision, showed that austerity didn't have to mean dowdiness and that women could still look smart within the coupon allowance.

Bazaar, 'Instead of Something New', pointed out that 'most of the model houses are pleased to redesign their old models for you' and showed how Digby Morton 'alters two of his last season's suits into a short-sleeved tweed dress with a velvet collar, and a jump suit.' But, if the writing was already on the wall for the women who patronised the top establishments, things were much more hopeful for the rest. Under the banner headline 'Why Women Will Find Dresses Scarce', the *Daily Sketch* pointed out that, out of 30,000 pre-war clothing factories only 1,500 were still functioning, and condoled with 'women out of uniform and mothers with families of growing girls' in their perplexity that there would soon be 'a smaller range of cloth and woven silks and no more fancy trimmings and adornments'. Although that sounded grim in a nation which, before the war, was estimated to be spending £260 million per year on clothes for women and children, in reality it was not. The reason was that, in order to utilise diminishing resources – human and material – in the fashion business, the government was finally forced to introduce the Utility scheme.

Hardy Amies adapted his pre-war tweed suits for the Board of Trade's Utility scheme with no great loss of style.

The government's thinking was simple: to create a range of clothes which was manufactured within strict guidelines and able to be purchased within the coupon schemes. It was no more sinister than that. The *Daily Herald* explained: 'The Board of Trade has no wish to adopt the role of fashion dictator. Fashion and the language of fashion no longer have a place in this war. The Board recognises, however, that the encouraging of good styling is one of the ways in which the government can assist the clothing industry. There is no intention of interfering with the styling of utility clothes by any manufacturer, provided he produces clothes which conform to the specification.' The scheme was immediately heralded by the press. 'Suburban wives and factory girls will soon be able to wear clothes designed and styled by the Queen's dressmaker,' the *Daily Mail* reported. The *News Chronicle* echoed, 'Before long the society woman who pays 30 guineas for a frock will share her dress designer with the factory girl who pays 30s.'

Women's magazines swung behind the new scheme with such a total commitment that it is

Cotton frocks and turbans, jazzed up with sunglasses, were as near to glamour as most women could hope to get.

hard not to imagine it as a response to government pressure to put a positive 'gloss' on the new situation. 'The backbone of morale is smartness,' *Harper's Bazaar* claimed. Wardrobe planning was put forward as a vital stratagem for survival: 'It's clever to give yourself a new wardrobe with two new blouses – only ten coupons.' Everyone was at pains to point out that this was not manipulation. Facing production and supply difficulties in a way that obviated the 'boom and bust' situation which a *laissez faire* approach would encourage, meant what was available could be shared fairly.

Initially, the Utility scheme covered 50 per cent of all cloth manufactured in Great Britain and controlled both its quality and price but, as the demand for uniforms meant that the War Office required even more, the total crept up to 85 per cent. Control soon bit harder. In May 1942 the first of a series of Civilian Clothing (Restrictions) Orders was imposed, beginning with men's dress. The amount of material which could be used on trimmings, pockets and trouser turn-ups was limited, as was the manufacture of socks.

In women's clothing, restrictions affected the number of pleats permissible in a skirt. A maximum width was laid down for belts, seams, collars and sleeves. No embroidery or ornamental stitching was permitted and fur and leather trims were banned. Although the saving in materials brought about by these measures was surely very small, the government persisted for two reasons. The first,

fitting in with the *Daily Herald*'s comment that fashion now had no place – repeated, amazingly enough, in *Harper's Bazaar*'s famous remark 'Fashion...is out of fashion...' – was psychological. While acknowledging the importance of dress for morale, it was determined to separate, for the very first time, smartness and fashionability. From now on, the two were not to be considered synonymous.

Such an approach could be seen as bizarre, striking as it did at the decorative urge, one of the well-springs of fashion. Women needed to be convinced that the restrictions would not make them look dowdy. The new approach required a hard sell and it got it by shifting emphasis: henceforth, lack of embellishment and narrowing of proportions were to be seen not as limiting but as liberating, for the first time enabling ordinary women to attain elegance by cutting away extraneous detail.

ABOVE AND LEFT: Tailored slim lines were practical, adaptable and required a minimum of material. A smart hat worked wonders. Cecil Beaton's sophisticated lens (above) managed to make even 'Utility' look glamorous.

RIGHT: The reality in the blitzed areas of major cities: women looking for replacement crockery had a much more ad hoc appearance.

Beaton's photograph of a Digby Morton suit against a bombed building justified *Vogue's* claim that 'fashion is indestructible'.

Not the easiest story to sell, but the government pulled it off by a brilliantly forward-looking coup which showed that an imagination was beating somewhere deep in the heart of Whitehall. Simplicity had long been the hallmark of the elegance of great couture. What better way to convince people that the Utility scheme was a positive and even desirable step than by bringing in London's couturiers to underwrite it? As the *News Chronicle* explained, 'The Board [of Trade] has invited fashion designers to prepare models of easy fitting, durable clothes which can be made in quantities. The idea is that the designs should give a lead in the use of simple practical models which will be attractive for those who wear them. The designs may be copied by all.' *The Times* added, 'Templates will be available to the trade, in various sizes, at a cost of 7s 6d for blouses and 10s 6d for costumes, overcoats and dresses.' A ceiling was put on the prices which retailers could charge for Utility clothes although, as the *Daily Mail* pointed out, it would depend on the materials available 'but the average prices will be: suit 92s 10d; coat 83s 7d; rayon dress 53s 7d; cotton dress 17s 10d; blouse 21s 5d.' *Women's Wear Daily* reported that British manufacturers were 'mad as hornets' at the restrictions and price structure, feeling that, with more consultation, they 'could have done better'.

But most people were happy enough with making the best of a difficult situation. The Utility Mark – two abstract-looking 'C' shapes dovetailed with 41, which stood for Civilian Clothing 1941 – was found on a range of twenty-eight Utility models, all to be sold at controlled prices. They were remarkably elegant and sophisticated, bearing out Molyneux's opinion that the restrictions were invaluable to British fashion because they forced on designers a discipline which made their clothes much less fussy than, in many cases, they had been before the war. Practicality – even severity – was the aim. Jackets were to have a prescribed number of buttons. High necks, small collars, sleeves without gathers or cuffs, double pockets and knee-length skirts were the basis for suits and dresses. Skirts could be gored or have an inverted pleat. It was the nearest thing to a civilian uniform for women in the history of dress. Women of fashion found the materials the most difficult thing to accept. Comparisons with sacking – made many times to Mass Observation collectors – were unfair, but the quality of wool mixtures available after the demand for uniforms had been satisfied was not high.

The press followed the government line and enthusiastically endorsed Utility garments. Fashion journalist Alison Settle commented on how much better dressed the workers would be. *Women & Beauty* thought the word Utility 'awful', but felt that a scheme that allowed 'poor people to buy clothes that are going to last' must be applauded. The *Daily Mail* did so in extravagant terms, giving Utility coats 'full marks for cut, material and finish!' and praising the authorities for using their imaginations. *Vogue*'s comment was 'They're Beauties! They're Utilities!' *Women & Beauty* pointed out the obvious flaw, which was that, even with prices pegged, the really poor would not be able to afford them as they had to spend all their coupons on 'shoddy boots and coats' which were the basic necessities, far removed from ideas of fashion.

At the launch of the scheme, Sir Thomas Barlow, the Director General of Civilian Clothing wrote in *Harper's Bazaar*:

> 'Very little publicity has been given to the programme, as from the national standpoint it is undesirable that anything should be said or done which would tend to stimulate the purchase of clothing, whether Utility or Non-utility. Our policy should rather be the exact opposite, namely, to encourage everybody to avoid purchasing clothes.
>
> 'By making do with the dress she has, a woman can free labour urgently required for making munitions or for other war purposes. There comes, however, a time when clothes cannot be repaired and it is necessary to buy new ones. Obviously she then wants to buy clothing of good coupon value at strictly controlled prices. It was for this purpose and to conserve and make use of the material available in the most effective manner possible that the Utility programme was devised. To turn over from free to controlled production is a very big undertaking, as it takes often six months at least to convert raw material into finished garments by virtue of the many processes through which it has to pass. Nevertheless, supplies of Utility clothing are already reaching the shops and the quantity available by the autumn will, we hope, be substantial.
>
> 'I must add that restrictions on the making of clothing are being worked out with the aid of trade panels who are helping the Board of Trade. The purpose of these restrictions is always towards simplification and the elimination of all ornament which has no relation to durability. It is true

'New Dresses for Old' was a seductive rallying cry. Achieving them was more problematical for most women.

that simplification and the reduction of the number of styles do reduce the variety of clothing to which we have been accustomed. Nevertheless, it is by no means the case that the restrictions proposed imply the production of what might be called a standard civilian uniform.

'If, then, I may sum up the position, my advice to your readers would be: Don't buy any clothes unless you must, and Utility clothing is the best purchased from the point of view of expenditure and coupon value.'

Other pieces of advice were 'to utilise every old garment before considering anything new...to realise that not using clothes coupons is saving the nation's labour and raw materials...to look after your uniforms as carefully as your civilian clothes.' Of course, the readership of *Harper's Bazaar*, like that of *Vogue* and *Tatler*, was almost entirely middle to upper class so the editorial content reflected the fact that ladies' maids were rapidly becoming a thing of the past and women who had never done a hand's turn were going to have to 'learn how to look after your clothes...find out the right way to wash and mend and iron' whilst still managing 'to keep a smiling face above the rag on your back' [sic]. It even suggested, 'If you're doing a lot of home laundering, invest in an ironing board.'

MAKE-DO AND MEND
says Mrs. Sew-and-Sew

Vogue had even more shocking advice for the previously pampered. Do it yourself reached an alarming point when it advised its readers to shampoo themselves and then went on comfortingly, 'Your face is probably not what it was. But don't despair. If you can't have treatments...clean it scrupulously, grease it regularly; use a patter, a moulder or even a spoon to work the cream well in...your hands probably tell a tale of hard work, coarse soap, lack of fats, inexperienced manicurists and cheap varnish...'

The Hon. Mrs James Rodney, writing in *Harper's Bazaar* as early as 1940, had pre-empted the advice in a piece called, hopefully enough, 'Capable Hands', illustrated by a photograph of the Countess of Huntington, accompanied by her cat, doing a little light gardening in her herbaceous border, immaculate hands well to the fore. Mrs Rodney explained why 'tell-tale' hands were already a problem, so early on in the war effort. Work on the land, in laboratories and munition factories, as well as 'working those acres ourselves in the newly acquired converted country houses' played havoc but 'it is a point of pride with the war worker to keep not only herself in as perfect physical condition as she can, but her hands as beautiful as possible...the care of the hands of the working woman in wartime is, if anything, more important than ever...' If for no other reason than for all the Make Do and Mend to come.

Make Do and Mend was introduced by the government because it was desperate to cut a consumer demand for clothes which could not be

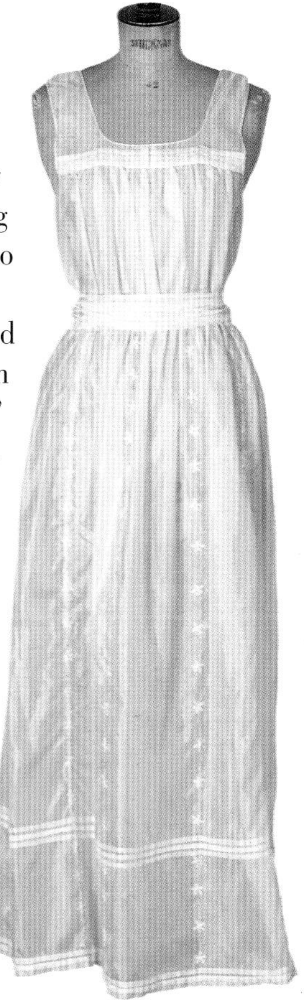

'War Time Needlework' did the same but went further, including knitting – possibly the commonest way of passing time during the whole period of the war – and how to make rugs from rags.

To the reader today – when few make and no one darns – the breadth of information seems both encyclopedic and arcane. 'Tips' abound. How to press – 'Never iron a corset'; 'Don't iron your stockings'; How to rescue – 'Stretched sweater necks can easily be re-conditioned'; How to substitute – 'Did you know that rice water can be used instead of starch?'; above all, how to be ingenious in darning (use net as a foundation), in sharpening scissors (work the blades on each side of a bottle neck), and even in ambitious projects like reblocking a felt hat (make a crown from cardboard). It was as if the entire female population of England had been conscripted into the Women's Institute.

How did ordinary women cope?

A surprising number took up the challenge and, emboldened by Make Do and Mend evening classes run by the WVS or WI, taught themselves at least the rudiments of home dressmaking. But, even with the skills, it wasn't easy. Fabric shortages had to be circumvented by any mean to hand. The result was more unique clothes on the streets than had ever been seen before. Coats made from blankets and travel rugs; dresses from twill black-out material; the rare piece of fabric brought home from abroad by someone in the services and – taking a leaf out of Scarlet O'Hara's book in *Gone With the Wind*, the most popular of films – even curtains which had been made redundant by black-out rules. Parachute silk, not easy to get hold of, legally or illegally, and used much less frequently than we now imagine, was very suitable for underwear as it could not be identified. Until 1945, when parachute material was put on sale, commandeering it was a crime. Although workers in parachute factories occasionally stole the odd length, for the majority of women who used it the supply was – as with so many other things – black market.

Not exactly made from old curtains, but this Vivien Leigh dress from *Gone With the Wind* encapsulated every woman's dreams.

Parachute silk, when available, could be used to make nightdresses and even wedding dresses in skilled hands.

Many women more or less turned their backs on appearance. They were far too busy. Those with men at the front preferred to spend their leisure

Many unique fashion statements resulted from using precious lengths of material with imagination, if not flair.

not in making clothes to feed what was seen as an impulse of vanity quite out of kilter with the sombre mood of the times but in knitting 'comforts' for the troops. Balaclavas, socks, mittens and scarves for fighting men seemed much more important than clothes for themselves. Of course, sweaters and scarves were knitted, using any colours available. 'No wool was ever thrown out,' I was told. 'No matter how little, it was unravelled and rolled up round a piece of paper or cardboard. You never knew when it would be handy.' Because they required little wool, fake sweater necks – 'just a roll collar and little dickie' – which could be made to look like a jumper under a suit or coat were popular, as were knitted cravats and jabots, for the same reason.

Although writers have romanticised the wartime knitting cult, depicting happy women, singly or in groups, sitting round a glowing fire darning, patching and knitting whilst listening to the radio, the reality was not so idyllic. Darning and patching – even if the right material could be found – were laborious, time-consuming and boring pastimes, far too difficult to be seen as a leisure pursuit by most women. Tired after work or single-handedly coping with children, all the women to whom I have spoken talked wearily of this aspect of Make Do and Mend as pure drudgery, forced on them by nothing but necessity. As one said with fervour, 'I swore, when it was all over, I'd never look at a pixie hood again.'

It wasn't just long days in dreary work which made women weary; it was also broken nights, 'being woken out of a sound sleep by the siren, staggering to the shelter and trying to keep warm and awake until the all-clear', that slowly sapped willpower and gnawed at self-esteem. This was the danger time when sisters, mothers and best friends had to pull each other up and say, 'Get smartened up, for God's sake! You don't want him coming back and finding you like this.'

They banded together in other ways. 'Sharing, swopping and second-hand' was how a Gloucestershire woman described the comradeship. Another, in Birmingham, commented that it was 'the big F that got us through. We were all on the fiddle in one way or another. You could get anything if you knew where to go. In 1943 I got a pair of silk cami-knickers – French – beautiful, just like pre-war, for a friend's trousseau. It was "no names, no pack drill". You always knew somebody who'd sell you the whole family's coupons if you wanted them.'

Spivs were there to help out and a woman who sold all her coupons didn't have to send her children to school without shoes. They were always available for cash if you went through the right – illegal – channels. 'Some

Rita Hayworth's long hair and seductively clinging evening dress were appreciated by both sexes, although they were beyond the realisation of women other than stars.

of the girls weren't too particular,' I was told by a woman in the North East. 'We knew the ones who were prepared to sleep with a man for some silk stockings or undies on the black market. No different to doing it with the Yanks, really.' Such attitudes were the exception. Although it is a fact that sexual morality was seen in a much freer light than in the Thirties, patriotism was so high that being immoral or unfaithful was not so much the crime. What really attracted social disapproval was trying to 'get one over on your friends'. One of the commonest, and most fervently believed, comments was 'As long as we're all in the same boat, we'll survive.' By trying to get more than your fair share you destroyed that.

The Harella label was noted for smart styling and workmanship.

It was a marvellous time for women to have sisters with whom to pool clothes. Niceties about colour, cut and style were forgotten as necessity took over. Initially, clothes were borrowed from family and friends only for special occasions, the most important of which were weddings, but as items wore out and could not be replaced the interchange became much more informal and regular. Sudden, inexplicable shortages of things previously in reasonable supply ('nothing was ever plentiful, you know, but some things could usually be had') would cause a problem.

In Gloucestershire, 'for about a year – I'm sure it was that long – you couldn't buy a hair net for love nor money. Knicker elastic, as well. That was always difficult.' Second-hand and pawnbroking establishments flourished – the first because there were no restrictions on second-hand goods and the second, ghoulishly enough, because many people in the poor areas of cities, having put things in, were killed in the Blitz or evacuated before they could retrieve them.

Evacuation could create its own fashion problems. It was very easy for a 'townie' to transgress local custom and raise hostility. With men in dwindling supply and the weekly hop not just the highlight but the only opportunity for fun, rivalry over appearance was intense. City girls were considered forward, not to say 'common'; they saw country girls as being as far back as Methuselah in morality, social behaviour and, above all, fashion sense. In *D for Doris, V for Victory*, Doris White recalls her time as an evacuee worker: 'One obvious difference was fashion,

As if to emphasise the difficulty of finding its products in the shops, Harella mounted a hugely successful Surrealist ad campaign, 'It's a Dream...'

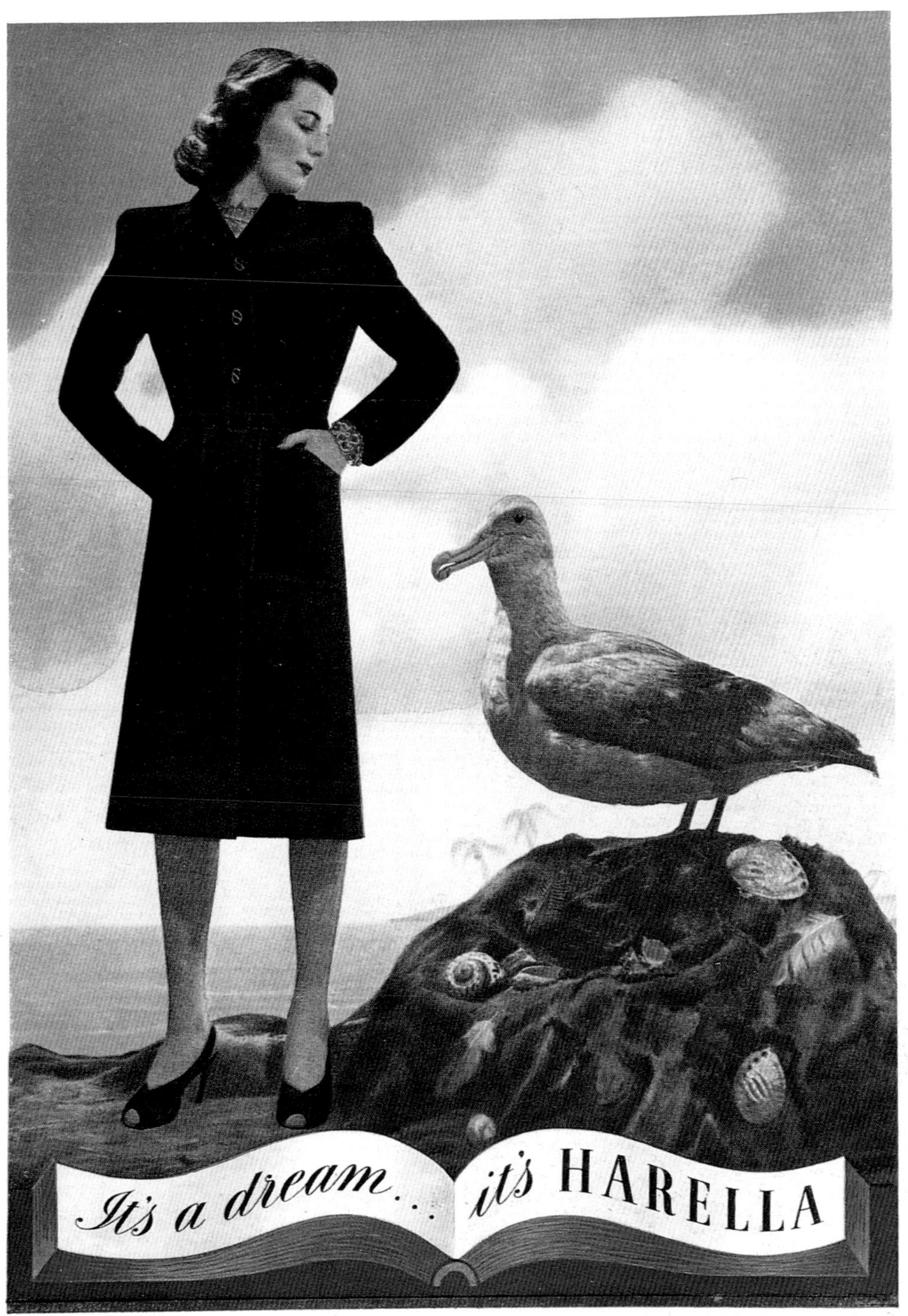

A town coat in Bouclé from Harella's Spring collection. Obtainable from all good fashion stores. If in any difficulty write to L. Harris Ltd. (wholesale only), 243 Regent Street, London, W.1.

Even a captured German flag could be transformed into a dressing gown.

YOUR SWEATERS. Preserve your ageing jersey for another winter, building it up with felt or leather, hiding its weaknesses with ribbons or bits of jewellery. Here again be bold about substituting; painted buttons decorate as well as beads. Long sleeves can be cut off at the elbow; so can short sleeves be lengthened, for warmth, with contrasting wool. Essential ingredients for this kind of cooking are imagination and taste.

When you take your sweater out to a party, wear a short necklace or even one of those old-fashioned chain bracelets sewn across the front, underlining the neck

If the buttonholes of your cardigan are frayed, edge the front with stiff ribbon and make new ones in this. Sew matching ribbon across the tops of the pockets and round the cuffs

Rejuvenate a sturdy country jersey by adding collar and patch pockets of natural wash-leather, stitched in the same colour as the sweater. Cut the collar from a good pattern

Wash-leather again—this time mounted in a yoke and as hip-pockets on a canary-yellow sweater which matches the colour of the leather as nearly as possible

Elbows are notorious weak spots of jerseys. Cut off long sleeves which are worn at the elbows and bind the raw edges with ribbon. Use more of the ribbon to outline a suggestion of a yoke and repeat the double line pattern on the sleeve

Here again, shortened sleeves are bound with ribbon, and adorned this time with frivolous bows. There's another bow on the high, square breast pocket

Another party trick: sew on to a plain sweater a triangular front of net bespattered with sequins or shiny beads. Shape the round of the neck and edge the net with a tiny rolled hem

In September 1942 even *Vogue* wasn't too grand to produce a 'Suggestions for Savings' edition.

which the country people gave little or no heed to... Glamour was all the rage for us girls, high heels, seamed stockings *and* suspenders, no lengths of elastic with knots for us. Hair was worn as long as possible, while country girls had theirs cut short... Shortages caused everyone to become devious... items we took for granted in peacetime conditions disappeared, like razor blades and hair clips.'

Every woman went to the pictures and had her favourite star, whose look she tried to copy. By far the most popular in the mid-war years was Rita Hayworth, whose healthy, gloriously coloured auburn hair, cascading down her back, brought sighs from women in the audience, only too aware that their shampoo was almost finished and they had no idea when the next consignment would appear. However, as one said, 'As long as we had our Tangee lipstick or some Cutex for our nails and some Lily of the Valley to splash on...it wasn't as if we weren't all in the same boat.' A touch of jewellery helped. Those who didn't have any and were working in factories often made their own brooches from offcuts of perspex or aluminium with a safety pin stuck on with aircraft glue. Country dwellers experimented, not always successfully, with acorns and beech nut, painted to match an outfit. Earrings were more problematic: many working-class girls thought them common and didn't wear them.

In all classes in the Thirties, Sunday had been a special day, for dressing up. For ordinary women 'Sunday Best' was very important. Whether going to church or just to see relatives, if they went out in public, they dressed formally. Hat, gloves, handbag – and umbrella, if necessary – had to 'tone', if not exactly match, and it was a serious fashion error to wear things that didn't 'go'. Inevitably, priorities changed. Sunday was just another day if you were working on a shift system. Even if you were still inclined to keep it special, the chances of preserving a fashionable appearance were virtually nil as things wore out and were not replaced. A formal coat or suit was the normal wear, especially for church. The coat had an especially powerful psychological significance for women as a proof of decency and social standing which has completely disappeared today, when many young women in particular don't even own a top coat and those who do would not consider it a bedrock foundation of their wardrobe.

In the Forties, when few owned a car and transport was frequently disrupted, a 'good' coat was a basic essential in every woman's wardrobe. It wasn't just the fact that the first two winters of wartime were exceptionally cold that made the problem of preserving – and, ultimately, replacing – their coats such a preoccupation with women. It was a question of respectability. Many women felt that there was something wanton about appearing publicly without one. 'When my mother's coat wore out under the arms,' I was told, 'she virtually became a prisoner in the house for a good part of the year. My aunts saved up and got her one in the end. You see, it would have been shaming for the whole family if she'd gone out with patches.'

Stories of men returning on leave to find their civvy suits no longer in the wardrobe but transformed and on a female back are common – and true. Many women cut up their husband's dressing gown to make a belted coat and some were ambitious enough to take his overcoats to cut down into an edge-

Jacqmar was in the ideological forefront with 'slogan' prints such as 'Dig for Victory'.

to-edge with a tie belt, swagger or three-quarter length coat – often with real success. It suddenly became an advantage to have a husband who was tall or even overweight, for the extra material you had. Make Do and Mend articles even explained how to do it. A smart suit could be made by a skilled needlewoman and, for those who were not up to it, a good dressmaker could work wonders.

Nothing was ever thrown away until it had finally worn out. Items of dress becoming 'tired' could often be given a new lease of life with a change of colour. But there were problems of which the cheerful magazine writers seemed unaware – possibly because they had never dyed anything. One woman recalls, 'My friend Dulcie always wanted to be into something new. She would have us dye this funny cream thing, like a cardigan, she'd got somewhere. We got a Drummer dye – only 1½d – bright red, it said, but it was more wine really. We did it in the small tin bath. it came out fine but, when it dried, it was – well, not *blotchy*, but not even. The worst was, the dye stained the bath. We didn't half get it! We were only sixteen!'

The major problem was that many dyes were fugitive and, if the garment had any hint of grease or wear, it didn't absorb at a uniform level. Streaks were inevitable – especially as almost by definition the items being dyed were not new. Drummer or Tintex ('25 lovely shades') dyes were good but not always generally available. Home-made substitutes were inevitably disastrous. Stephen's blue/black ink stained underwear if dampened by sweat and immediately ran if exposed to rain. Attempts to dye or paint shoes black were always ill-fated. Half an hour waiting for a bus in the rain turned stockings and feet blue. But failures could rarely be cast aside. At least a woman was trying to keep up appearances. 'It was the biggest crime of all to let yourself go,' a woman who organised evacuees says. 'You could always tell the ones who were really homesick and unhappy because they became slipshod. Being shabby didn't matter. We were *all* that. It was something more. A carelessness. We looked out for it in the young mothers. It was a sign.' An ordinary countrywoman puts the other side: 'We were all a bit down at heel, but never scruffy. "All clean and paid for," we used to say. You couldn't let yourself become a slattern just because of old Hitler.'

A dressing gown made from material printed with maps of the British Isles and the slogan 'This England'.

Respectable women, like fashionable women, were unhappy without a hat, although younger ones were delighted to toss theirs aside and become part of the general move towards a look which, following the stars, emphasised the hair. But all women in uniform had to cover their hair whilst on duty, as did workers in factories. The

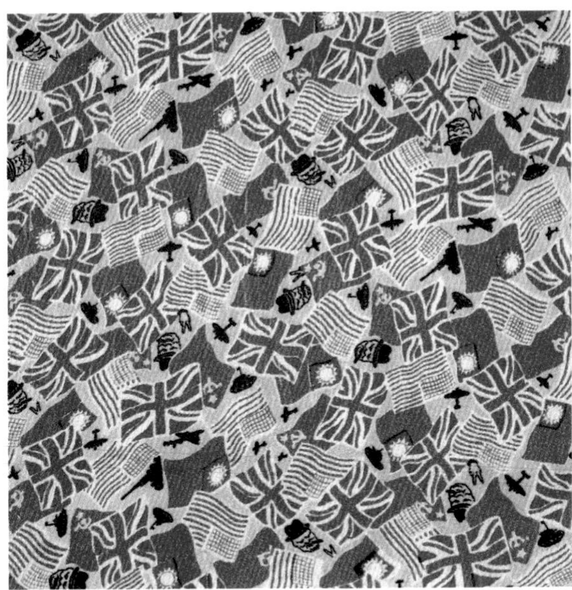

Victory was the slogan that never failed to sell. This 'Victory' print was much in demand with home dressmakers.

turban, which rapidly became as ubiquitous as the dark cotton pinny with brightly coloured flowers on the streets and doorsteps of the poorer quarters, was normally made from a scarf wrapped around the head, although many women bought them. Made of jersey, they could be rolled up and stuffed in a pocket, but lasted for a remarkable time.

Women who did not like the turban covered their heads with a head scarf which had become a fashion, for young women in particular, at the beginning of the war. Jacqmar's scarves, introduced in 1940, were considered the best, although not all women could afford them. While the Queen was never seen in any item of dress so informal, royal watchers date the love affair with the head scarf which both her daughters have had all their lives, from their formative years in the Forties.

In 1942 Jacqmar's designer, Arnold Lever,

produced a range of prints which were made up into clothes by the designer Bianca Mosca to be worn by prominent women for propaganda photographs. The fabric of Lady Beatty's blouse was called 'The Navy's Here'. Ellen Wilkinson, Parliamentary Secretary to the Ministry of Home Security, wore 'Fall-in the Firebomb Fighters'; Mrs Robert Hudson, wife of the Minister of Agriculture, had an apron in 'Dig For Victory' and Lady Portal, whose husband was the Chief of Air Staff, was photographed in the 'Happy Landing' print. Actresses were brought in for glamour. Vivien Leigh's blouse was made from the '66 Coupons' print – referring to the number allocated to adults per year – which was scattered with rare and rationed items; Frances Day's playsuit was covered in posters extolling the war effort and ENSA star Claire Luce wore 'Home Guard' pyjamas – not quite Betty Grable in a swimsuit, but nevertheless excellent for morale.

As were hats. Many women felt that they were the only item of clothing left which could give their appearance some personal style. But the old bugbear, shortage of raw materials, affected them as it did all clothes manufacture. Straw became difficult to get. Later, felt became scarce. Prices went up – as they could because hats, being outside the coupon system, were not subject to government control. Most ordinary women were forced to make their own. Turbans, pixie hoods and snoods – invented by Schiaparelli to enclose the hair in a glamorously medieval manner – were popular. Magazines carried instructions for knitted or crocheted bonnets, tam-o-shanters and berets, usually with matching gloves or mittens, but none was sufficiently ingenious to come up with an idea that raised their pattern above the drab and dull quality inherent in the shapes themselves. For hats to flatter, clever needlewomen looked elsewhere. They turned for sound practical advice to the many manuals of millinery available.

One of the most popular in the Boot's lending library was Amy J. Reeve's *Practical Home Millinery*, originally published in 1912 and still going strong thirty years on. Essentially down to earth, illustrating each step with clear diagrams, it is easy to understand its popularity. Its 'Renovations' section was full of valuable information which went beyond suggestions on cleaning felt or straw and included separate instructions for sprucing up black and white lace. Its advice for dealing with furs strikes modern readers as slightly alarming – 'Sable and fox may be cleaned with hot bran'; 'Saturate some sawdust with benzoline or petrol and rub well into the fur'; 'Brush well with Scrubbs' Ammonia before shaking before the fire'; – but it is a reminder of how keen women were to hang on to their fur coats, no matter how old or dilapidated, not for swank but for warmth.

A 'dressy' hat was for both – and more. Modern women find it difficult to imagine how much status was wrapped up in hats. Shortly after the war, Madame Eva Ritcher, a Mayfair milliner, wrote her *ABC of Millinery*. No one found any inconsistency in the introduction, by the respected novelist and intellectual Elizabeth Bowen, claiming that hats were an art; her tribute to them and to the milliner's skills was considered perfectly fit and proper.

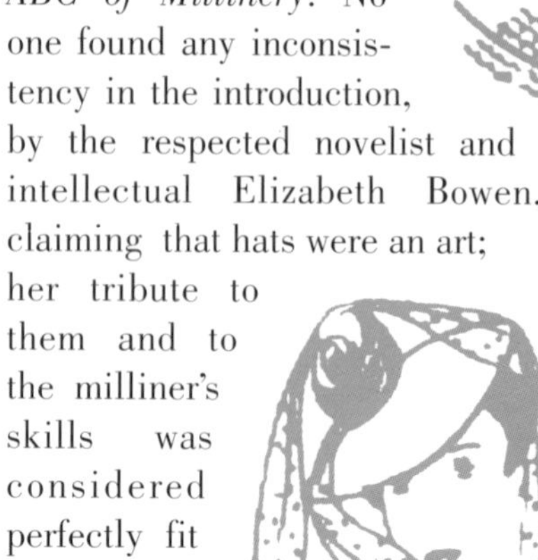

Keeping essential items of dress in good repair was vital. Women's magazines were full of advice on fabric care and articles stressing the importance of careful laundering. In the days before washing machines and spin dryers, washing clothes was hard but drying them even harder. especially in the winter when the indoor clothes horse had to substitute for the outside clothes line. 'Our mum used to boil everything up in the copper,' one woman recalls. 'I can smell that Monday soap-sud smell now. Then she'd put them through the mangle. I was the eldest so I had to help turning the handle. It was hard.' Oxydol soap powder not only had notes on the packet – 'Mrs Mundy's Helping Hand' – to advise the best way to use it, the company, Thomas Hedley & Co, took advertising space in newspapers and magazines to dispense 'Make Do and Mend Washday Wisdom' with 'Busy Bubble's Helping Hand': 'It's no good making up new clothes from old material unless you make sure they last,' they proclaimed. 'Fabrics certainly won't stand up to hard rubbing and scrubbing in the washtub. Use Oxydol, the amazing granulated soap.'

Reading the advertisements and buying the goods were different things. Shopping, once a pleasure and relaxation, presented great problems during the war. Women on war work put in long shifts in factories and, of course, were normally working during the hours when shops were open. Various ways were found to overcome the difficulty. Most firms arranged for time off, ranging from two 'shopping break' hours per week to half a day.

Queues were the problem for all women. Invariably long and slow-moving, they were nevertheless compulsive. A queue mentality developed as the war went on. People joined virtually any line the moment it began to form and often didn't bother to ask what they were queuing for. The woman who said, 'If you saw it, you bought it,' spoke for thousands who knew that whatever the commodity, the chances were that they would have run out of it at home long ago.

It was necessary to queue for everything rationed, and therefore in limited supply, and the whisper 'They've got something in' had

Maps printed on silk, like this one of China, were a way of finding pattern in an era when, for ease of production, much of the available material was plain.

women converging immediately. But the system worked against those released from factories for only a limited time and in many districts they were issued with priority cards by their employers, in agreement with the shopkeepers who, in any case, always kept things 'under the counter' for regulars even if they couldn't always queue. Other ways round the problem were to allow key workers to register in advance for rationed goods and even to enrol older women to act as professional shoppers for the factory girls in order that production could continue uninterrupted. It was psychologically sound for both sets of women. As a magazine editorial pointed out, 'The older woman is needed to take the place of those who can be more usefully employed in an active capacity...let the older woman realise that this is her moment, that it is up to her to...set an inspiring standard of self-command and self-confidence to those younger who will unconsciously benefit by her good example.' Not even the government could have put it better. Behind the words lurked the unspoken acknowledgement that not all women were coping as well as they seemed, and an acceptance that it was not just the Blitz that gave them the blues!

Queuing quickly became a way of life. Evelyn Dunbar's painting of the fish queue shows a scene to be found in every town and village.

At the back of every woman's mind, running as a constant theme behind all her other daily worries, was the clothes question. Things were getting worse by the month. There was so little of anything available that it was strangely encouraging to learn of the problems of other women in Europe. Comfort could be had from the interview with the Belgian refugee who reported that, in her country, although the coupon allowance was generous, buying new clothes was pointless because the materials were so bad. Worst was a kind of wool made from dried milk, which melted in the heat. Dresses were endlessly turned; new ones were created from bedspreads and curtains but even that was difficult as there was a chronic dearth of sewing machines. The worst of all shortages, not only in Belgium but across Europe generally, was leather. As only people with special workers' permits were allowed to buy shoes, most of the population wore heavy wooden sabots. Some even tried to make their own from old leather handbags and suitcases. Dressmakers were kept busy renovating old clothes for their customers.

They were no less so in England. Peter Jones and John Lewis advertised a renovation service

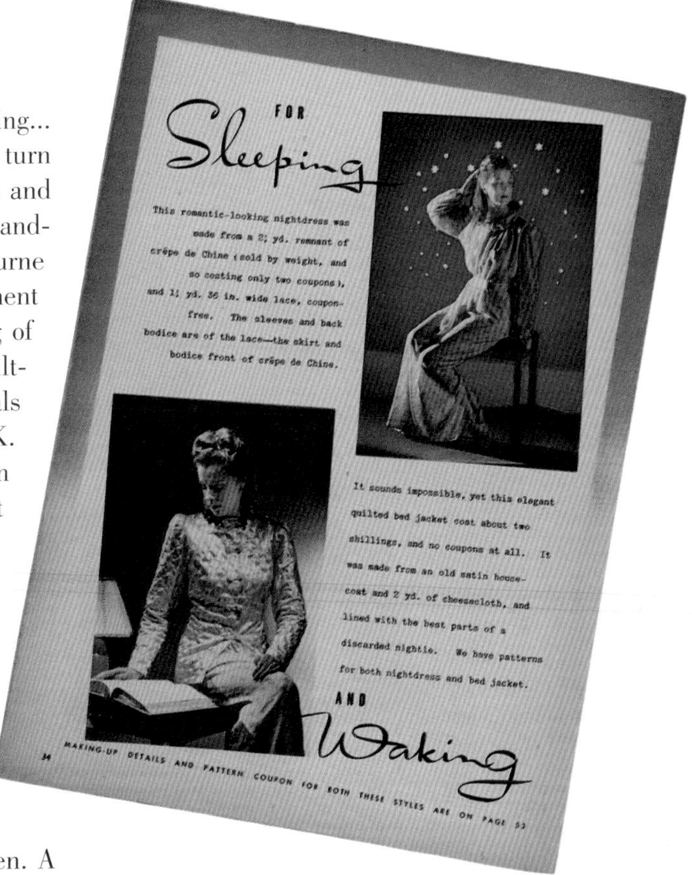

FOR
Sleeping

This romantic-looking nightdress was made from a 2½ yd. remnant of crêpe de Chine (sold by weight, and so costing only two coupons), and 1½ yd. 36 in. wide lace, coupon-free. The sleeves and back bodice are of the lace—the skirt and bodice front of crêpe de Chine.

It sounds impossible, yet this elegant quilted bed jacket cost about two shillings, and no coupons at all. It was made from an old satin house-coat and 2 yd. of cheesecloth, and lined with the best parts of a discarded nightie. We have patterns for both nightdress and bed jacket.

AND
Waking

34 MAKING-UP DETAILS AND PATTERN COUPON FOR BOTH THESE STYLES ARE ON PAGE 53

that 'will undertake to do almost everything... make a dress out of a pair of flannel trousers... turn evening gowns into day dresses, men's suits and shirts into women's suits and blouses...mend handbags, repair hinges, recover and re-line.' Bourne & Hollingsworth, whose dressmaking department had become noted for its clever remodelling of clothes, was offering 'similar miracles upon wilting hats' by 1943, when hats and the materials to make them were becoming scarce. The K. Dressel Reconditioning Service, 'well known for mending ladders invisibly, will re-foot stockings'. You sent in three pairs and received two back.

Queens have different problems. Wishing to show not only sympathy but also solidarity with women who had been blitzed, Queen Elizabeth discussed the question of colour with Hartnell. What would be suitable for situations where people were devastated and often bereaved? Black was out of the question. She embargoed green. A tactful choice was made by choosing pinks, lilacs and blues, all subdued and muted.

Although couturiers continued to show clothes – or, at least, have them photographed for the magazines – the top end of the market was as stagnant as everywhere else. As with mass production, there weren't enough hands. As *Vogue* reported in 1943, 'Every designer tells the same tale. His staff is down to a fraction of its former strength...his customers are still ordering and his workrooms still making the models from his *previous* collection.' The Queen's milliner, Aage Thaarup, had realised early on that many of his customers would move to the country to avoid the bombing. To keep his workrooms ticking over, he began a mail-order scheme: 'If you will send your photograph in your favourite old hat with a sample of the colour you want,' he promised, 'I will send back sketches and models made in canvas. Upon receipt of your choice I will forward the finished hat within three days. If you don't like it, you can send it back.'

In January 1943 *Women's Wear Daily* reported the craze for 'reconfectioning' in London, started by the actress Evelyn Laye, who brought in to Hartnell a dress which she had bought in America before the war. He modernised the dress by removing the frills. As *Women's Wear Daily* said, this 'saved enough material to make a doll for a war charity and leave Miss Laye with a new dress and her coupons intact.' In fact, it was no novelty – apart from the charity doll. Every dress house in the country was reconfectioning for

Magazine editors were adept at photographing clothes for home dressmakers to bring out their glamour.

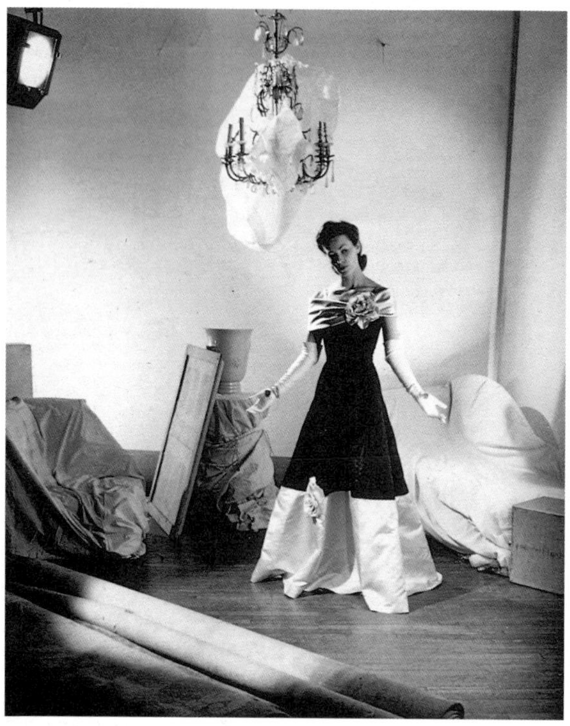

The drive for export dollars kept London high fashion alive, as can be seen in this Molyneux ballgown of 1941.

customers. The few new dresses that were being designed were, according to *Women's Wear Daily*, as likely as not left to elderly vendeuses to make. 'There is no seasonal element,' the newspaper's London office reported, 'because the clothes take too long to make.'

Increasingly, women could only dream of new clothes. Fashion magazines had a double message. Virtually all dresses which were shown without a price or coupon value – at least a third of the editorial images per month – were not available. Reserved for export, they were featured for the foreign trade, in an attempt to keep their interest in British goods. Dresses shown without designer or manufacturer details were almost always American clothes, pictures of which were brought in to fill the pages. The clothes which could be bought were subject to availability and magazines always carried the rider 'Owing to prevailing conditions, it is hoped that readers will understand it is not always possible to guarantee that the actual merchandise pictured in these pages is available everywhere.' The whole editorial approach was dictated by the conviction that, despite all, the role of the fashion magazine in time of war was to keep fashion desire alive.

Fashions like these were artfully photographed to attract foreign customers to London couture.

In this, magazines were running a two-fold risk. Although the idea behind showing beautiful, unattainable clothes was to keep hope, and therefore morale, high, it could have a counter effect. As an old friend told me, 'I gave up looking at magazines. There wasn't any point. Nothing could be had. It just irritated me to see all these pictures of glamorous women when I didn't even have any face cream.' Apart from alienating many readers, magazines were often in danger of running counter to the government's plans. Quite simply, the two were walking different paths. Magazine editors had been so behind all government edicts that they gave even restrictions their vociferous support. But, by the mid-war point, they were beginning to question much that seemed counterproductive to a situation where maintaining female morale was essential. Having featured 'Get Together and Dig' parties (with appropriately chic gardening clothes from Lillywhite and Heathercraft), *Harper's Bazaar* even lined up behind the government sufficiently to advise its readers, renowned for their grandeur, to 'carry your own string bag'. Slogans for savers were scattered throughout the pages: 'Buy War Savings Certificates'; 'Invest in War Loans'; 'Become a Collector for the Penny a Week Fund'. But none of this was enough for the government.

It created the 'Squander-Bug' as a graphic, cartoony way of trying to convince women that they

Children's Shoe & Clothing EXCHANGE

One of the best ways to obtain new clothing was to swap – especially if things were outgrown before they were outworn.

must not waste money on clothes purely for vanity or whim. The National Savings Committee flooded magazines with the crudest propaganda.

'The Squander-Bug Works for Hitler!' the advertisements screamed. 'When your Savings Group Secretary calls, there's always a third party present. The little Saboteur, the Squander-Bug...he hates to see money going to help the boys who are fighting...' The more sophisticated woman found it slightly risible. 'I used to think it a waste of money,' one told me. 'The advertising, I mean. Even if you had the cash, there was hardly anything to spend it on!'

Even when people could buy, shopping was not what it had been. In the winter, shops opened later and closed earlier to save on lighting and heating. The drive to save paper meant that goods were not allowed to be wrapped unless they were being sent or delivered. Personal shoppers had to bring their own or carry their purchases away unwrapped. With the imposition of Purchase Tax in 1940, everything had become dearer. It was a relief in 1942 to have Purchase Tax removed from all Utility goods except furs and fully fashioned stockings – despite the Treasury's concern at the lost revenue brought about by such a concession.

Everyone was aware of the problem. The government tried its best to keep morale and, above all, hope high by a mixture of congratulation, instruction and advice for the women of Britain, always delivered with the unspoken assurance that all the horrors, difficulties and privations were temporary. In 1943, Government Minister Hugh Dalton made a straightforward appeal to patriotism when he thought female spirits were flagging. *Good Housekeeping* printed his letter, 'To All of You' in which he praised and encouraged:

> 'Two years of clothes rationing have come and gone. There are 600,000 fewer workers making civilian clothes...a saving of manpower of which we can all be proud. To all of you who have cheerfully made-do, who have mended and managed... I say – thank you.
>
> 'Remember that every coupon unspent means less strain on the country's resources. To wear clothes that have been patched and darned – perhaps many times – is to show oneself a true patriot... Making do may at times seem a little dreary... But, even when old clothes aren't exciting, they are a war-winning fashion to follow which will speed the day of victory.'

Such a straightforward anti-consumer message was a hard pill to sugar for fashion magazines whose whole *raison d'être* was consumerism, but they managed to speak with forked tongue remarkably successfully. They would not have dreamed of opposing the government's tactics. Like everybody else, editors and publishers knew the wisdom of the exhortations. But, in a way in which governments do not, they understood how vital to female morale appearance was. It wasn't just a question of wanting to look pretty, although that was an important consideration when boyfriends and husbands were returning from the services so briefly and frequently with no warning. It was much more deeply embedded in the female culture that had been evolving for over a hundred years: the role of a woman was seen by many as being inextricably linked with buying. Free thinkers and intellectuals found the idea of such narrow parameters reprehensible, and they were right to do so. But the difficulty facing women, government and editors as shops closed or were bombed out and supplies dwindled to absurd levels was that a huge prop to morale had been removed and no substitute could be found, no matter how hard everyone pushed the joys of Make Do and Mend.

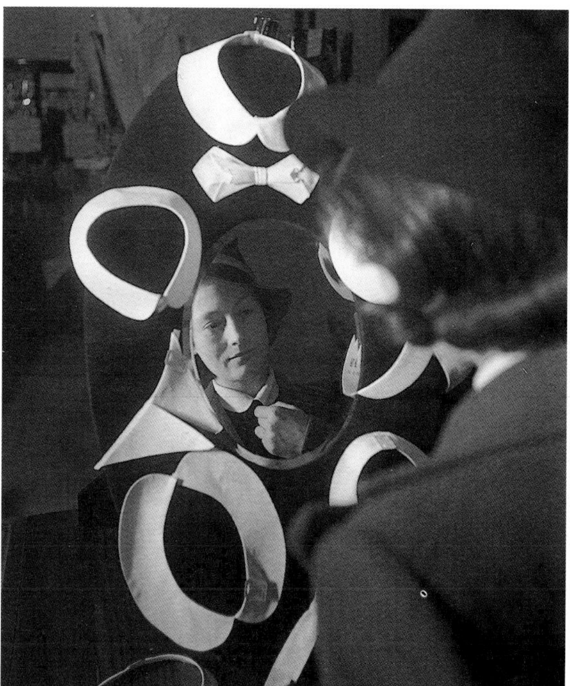

Black-out restrictions meant that wearing white after dark was encouraged, even it was just a collar or a belt.

Looking back, the sustained cheerfulness is moving testimony to the belief the women of Britain had in the goodness of the fight and the importance of their part in it. Pragmatism was the approach to all things. When hats became scarce and the President of the Board of Trade asked the Archbishop of Canterbury to announce that going hatless to church was not improper, there was an upsurge of Sunday head scarves. 'Even if you had hats,' I was told, 'in our village we stopped wearing them. It didn't seem right to show off. Head scarves made us all the same.'

With chronic shortages of leather, an attempt was made to introduce clogs. They were government issue to war workers, at £1 15s per pair, in beige, their uppers fixed to the sole with brass studs. Hideous, heavy and as noisy as they were uncomfortable, the wooden soles were to be worn, according to *Vogue*, 'rocking from heel to toe'. More refined – and expensive – versions were designed to make walking less tiring by having a hinged sole which opened with each step. But clogs never caught on and were quietly dropped. Not one of the many women I talked to whilst researching this book had ever owned a pair or knew of anyone who did. Wooden-soled shoes had too many peasant connotations in the popular mind. Reminding people of slavery and defeat, they were at variance with the up-beat mood the country needed. And victory required shoes. In the end, to try to beat the leather shortages gabardine was increasingly substituted in woman's shoes, as felt was used for handbags, in order to keep the spirit, even if an illusion.

Many unwary fashion commentators have assumed, because clogs were featured in newspapers and magazines, that they were a fashion. They were not. Even during wartime difficulties, it must be remembered that fashion requires consensus. The same caution must be brought to bear when examining the role of clothes in the black-out – or the Big Dim, as the Americans called it. Popular magazines carried pictures of people wearing white so that they would show up in the dark. Some even showed pictures of men with their white shirt-tails hanging below their suit jackets and many featured pictures of women painting jewellery or replacing coloured buttons with white. Possibly some did, but the vast majority of women had more vital things on which to spend their time and they viewed the pictures of black-out ideas as amusingly ingenious but not for them.

Gas-mask practices were encouraged even in public places like this store in Bayswater, but how seriously they were taken away from the publicity cameras is another thing altogether.

Some things were too severely controlled to be left to personal whim. We all know about black-out – 'Put That Light Out' – and the fact that place names on stations and on signposts were obliterated. In dress, it was gas masks which people were forced to take seriously. They were to be carried at all times in public places. To begin with, the threat of chemical war – seemed so great that the public willingly co-operated. The gas mask became an automatic part of a woman's outfit, stimulating a fashion fad for shoulder bags so that, if the mask had to be put on in a hurry, a woman didn't need to waste time trying to find somewhere to put her handbag. Inevitably, when the gas attacks failed to come, people became slack. In the country, especially, gas masks had always been an encumbrance, actively interfering with efficiency, and they eventually disappeared, with the tacit agreement of police and magistrates. As information about the German war effort became clearer, it was obvious that gas masks were

unlikely to be required and they were quietly forgotten about, like much that had seemed important in the 'Phoney War' of 1939.

By the middle of 1943, a quiet revolution had taken place in women's dress. A combination of rationing and radically modified attitudes had eroded much of the formality of the prewar years. Stockings, hats and gloves – 'black suede is a thing of the past' – were no longer *de rigueur*, as they had been. The 'correct' shoes, such an obsession of magazines in the Thirties – 'A lady can always be recognised by the shoes she wears and the state they are in' – were now any shoes a woman had. If they were down-at-heel – a totally reprehensible thing previously – that was regrettable but understandable. There were no restrictions on bringing shoes from abroad, and husbands and boyfriends frequently produced the coveted brand-new pair from their leave kit-bags. Some even tried to make shoes for their womenfolk. It was easy to buy a wedge-heel shaped base – often of cork – and make straps from electrician's tape, fine rope (although that could cut into the skin) and strips of old leather salvaged from shoes beyond repair. Overcoming the leather shortage inspired some of the most imaginative self-help of the war.

Top stores made a virtue from necessity and produced a range of superior 'comforts' to make shelter life less of an ordeal.

Leather wasn't the only thing in short supply. There were few cobblers and, even if one could be found, the wait involved in even simple repairs was daunting. Phillips Stick-A-Soles and Phillips Heels carried encouraging advertisements advising how to spend less on shoes, 'even with prices so high' in which a housewife tells her friend, 'It's so difficult to keep off money worries when I write to Jack... Shoes, for instance, it's terrible how much they cost...' A quick word in her ear and, three months later, with the shoes of the whole family protected by Phillips, money worries are solved. It wasn't always so easy.

For many women, the hardest thing to cope with was the effect of shortages and increased costs on the one occasion when clothes really mattered: their wedding day. Marriage during the war took on a heightened emotional and social significance, symbolising as it did the continuity of basic values which no amount of demoralisation or uncertainty could undermine. The traditional white wedding with a church ceremony was every woman's dream, but it frequently had to be trimmed in order to fit into

A 1939 designer's idea for a handbag with built-in gas-mask compartment.

Miniature Portable Battery Radio £9.9.0
Electric Shelter Lamp with own charger—use all night—charge all day on ordinary electric light socket £3.3.0
Grey Woollen Mittens with coloured stripes 7/9
Thermos Jars from £2.2.0
THERMOS
Gold Identity Bracelets from £3.5.6. Silver, from £1.1.0
Prices include engraving name and address.
Woollen Ribbed Long Sleeved Jersey 45/-
COMFORTS
for the shelter
If we have to shelter, then let us shelter as comfortably as possible! If we're inclined to sleeplessness, then let us make the sleep we get as reposeful as we can.
• The House of Fortnum & Mason are accustomed to catering for the greater comfort of their clients, in all emergencies. Here, we hope, you agree that a number of practical suggestions are made in this direction.
Our Camel Hair Sleeping Bag costs 14 Gns., but is the last word in comfort—it is lined with lamb's wool and has detachable sheets. OTHERS from £3.15.0.
GoldenCrocodile Pocket Flask, with silver cup £4.14.6. Others from 32/6
F & M
FORTNUM 182 PICCADILLY, W.1 MASON
Cigars from £5 per 100 to £20 per 100
Fancy Boxes of Chocolates from 15/6
Spotted Wool Jersey Tailored Pyjamas £6.6.0. Three-quarter length tailored coat to match £6.6.0

the new circumstances. Even the ring wasn't always easy to come by. Several women told me that they had to put their names down on a waiting list for many months, even though they were not sure of the exact date of the wedding, and one recalls that she was forced to borrow her mother's ring for the ceremony. In contrast with the long-term planning normally given to weddings, wartime ones were often helterskelter affairs sparked by a telegram out of the blue saying that the bridegroom was coming home on a forty-eight-hour pass. Someone rushed to the registrar or a clergyman for a licence while the bride organised her dress.

Inside the shelters, life went on. Here, friends 'do' each other's hair to pass the time.

Circumstances frequently – but by no means always – made dreams of a white wedding a thing of the past. As early as June 1940, a wedding feature in *Harper's Bazaar* showed suits, dresses and bolero outfits, but no traditional brides' dresses. Many women settled for being married in their smartest day clothes. Those in the forces, especially if commissioned and marrying a man in the services, could wear their uniform, although this was rare for an occasion when most women wished to look their feminine best. Normally, a white wedding was contrived in some way or another – often, of course, by borrowing a pre-war dress. To buy a new one was barely viable with the coupon situation, although some were available. Prices started at about £4 and could go beyond £20, although most cost little more than £8. In 1944, Derry & Toms advertised a dress in rayon satin for £13 15s 6d and seven coupons. The traditional Thirties' 'bridal satin', woven with a fine, small flower, not unlike damask, was totally unobtainable although, for a daughter of a local pillar of society, 'pre-war quality' could often be discovered 'under the counter'.

But an emphasis on grandeur was inappropriate. Even with whole families saving their points, practicality normally prevailed and the coupons were put towards a trousseau. At least those clothes could be worn again, whereas a wedding dress, although it could be dyed afterwards, had a limited life. By 1942, even those women who before the war had been in the habit of dressing for dinner or wearing evening gowns had stopped doing so. It seemed frivolous when so many were making sacrifices, and frivolity had come to be equated with disloyalty to the cause.

White weddings did not all rely on borrowing. Curtain lace, which was not part of the points system, could be used to make a long dress, worn with a white nightdress underneath. It was also used for the veil, unless one could be borrowed or hired.

The happy couple had to carry gas masks and walk through an arch of sandbags, but they were still dressed in their best for this non-white wedding at the beginning of the war.

Buying one meant joining a long waiting list – at least nine months in one Midlands town. Those who *did* make their wedding dresses invariably gave them narrow skirts, to save on material. If they were cutting a dress from parachute silk, they had the extra problem that it came in thin, elongated triangles and needed to be cut on the cross – a difficult thing for a professional, let alone a home dressmaker. Square necklines and tight-fitting sleeves, slightly puffed at the shoulders were very popular, although romantics favoured necklines scooped into a heart shape. There was rarely material to spare for draping or shirring. The bodice, like the skirt, was cut as tight as modesty allowed. All too often the end result looked skimpy. Gloves, frequently crocheted from white cotton, were an extra refinement.

Life during the war was far from even. Countrywomen had advantages when it came to staple foods such as eggs and vegetables. But, when it came to dress, the winner was usually the woman in the town. Whether making a wedding dress or assembling a trousseau, she was more likely to be able to buy coupons illegally – many from books registered in the names of people killed or missing in the Blitz – and then find the right spiv or market stall for the fabrics required.

By 1943, a new mood had taken hold and it was generally considered inappropriate to have a white wedding. From then until well into the post-war years, it was perfectly acceptable to be married in day clothes – normally a suit and a very smart hat. Although some women probably felt deprived of a traditional birth-right, from my research it would appear that the majority felt liberated and, above all, modern when they walked down the aisle in a short skirt.

'Trousseau for a War Bride', created by an art student in 1940, featuring two snoods, a turban, a detachable coat hood and a muff.

It is a measure of the inroads made into fashion by the war and its attendant tribulations that, by 1944, most women's preoccupation with personal appearance was not with their dress but with how to keep themselves looking beautiful. Toiletries were so scarce that it was the cause of much joy if a woman could get her hands on a bottle of drene shampoo, endorsed by such stars as Googie Withers and Greta Gynt, and absolute delirium if her local chemist profferred a Christy Natural Wave which promised to transform 'straight-as-a-poker hair into glorious natural waves – waves that grow as your hair grows, that will last through the years to come'.

With dreams of such small delights, the women of Britain limped – but resolutely and even happily – towards the final war years, the lucky ones sporting 'the Freedom Cut', contrived by Raymond of Mayfair, their hair – short, waved and off the forehead – giving them the look of keen, workmanlike vigour that the government and magazines had worked so assiduously to promote.

TROUSSEAU FOR A WINTER
WAR BRIDE.
Barbara Gals.
Winter 1939 – 1940
Woollen dress and jacket.
Blue gloves & draped hat.
Peach net snood.
Peach velvet and gorgette housecoat.
Feathered mules
Black felt hat
White organdie blouse.
Blue woollen jumper with sequins.
Green velvet dinner gown.
Gold snood
Gold sequined handbag.
Black gloves & handbag.
Black shoes.
Smart black coat for Town.
Black velvet turban.
Blue sandles.
White fur cape
Grey swagger coat (with a detachable hood) and a grey costume.
Rose pink angora jumper.
Green hat and gloves.
Black brogues.
Blue gorgette gown with sequins on the skirt.

Vogue
INCORPORATING VOGUE BEAUTY BOOK,
VOGUE HOUSE AND GARDEN BOOK
PARIS SPRING FASHIC
WITH VOGUE PATTERN BC
MARCH 1940 (3) • PRICE

CHAPTER 4

Other Frontiers, Other Dreams

Left: A hat to lift the spirits. Above: Understated elegance from Balenciaga.

If by the mid-war years British fashion had almost died for most women it was alive, if not entirely well, abroad. In fact, high fashion had become entirely a thing for export as clothes were used as unlikely ammunition in the struggle for the US dollars so vital to the war effort.

It was a war, or at least a battle, which had been going on long before Hitler made his final move. The fight was over who would command the world fashion trade. The protagonists were France, Britain and America. The target was the still fledgling world of top quality ready-to-wear which was eventually to develop into the designer label industry of our own time. The issue was the fashion hegemony of Paris.

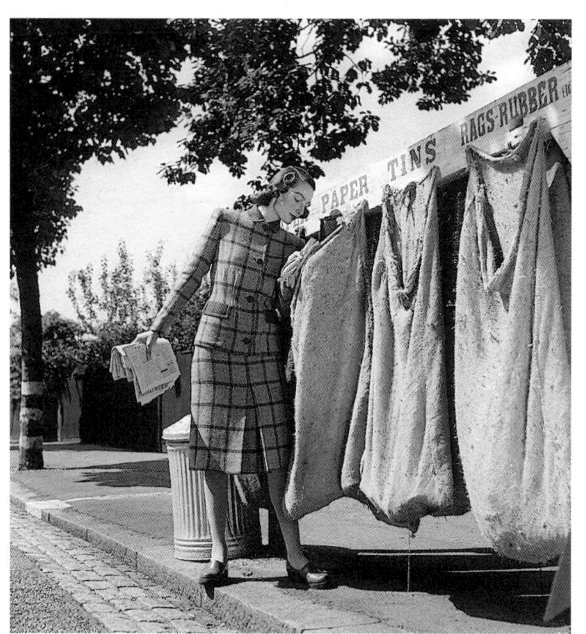

ABOVE AND RIGHT: *Vogue* got behind the salvage drive by photographing 'collectors' in the latest fashions.

Two of the most persistent fashion myths of this century are that the Americans invented ready-to-wear fashion and that they alone keep Paris couture viable. In fact, ready-made clothes have been a feature of fashion since the seventeenth century. It was the mechanisation brought by American manufacturers at a crucial point in the second half of the nineteenth century which made it an industry. Couture has always been predominantly a French approach to dress. On average this century, sales of French couture to America have accounted for less than ten per cent of normal annual turnover. And yet, both myths continue.

Ready-to-wear has long made a major contribution to the US economy. As early as 1837, a year of financial depression in the US, ready-made clothing accounted for $1.7m worth of trade in Boston, compared to $756,000 from copper workings and $652,000 from ship-building. And of the clothing total by far the majority was generated by hats, shoes and boots.

America had the industry but what it felt it lacked was the inspiration. For this, it turned to Paris. Even in 1828 a Boston merchant was advertising 'French' ready-to-wear dresses. Thirty years later, New York was renowned for the speed at which it could reproduce *le dernier cri* from the City of Light. Even in London, manufacturers were boasting that their Paris copies were not only quickly available, they were selling more cheaply than the originals in the couture capital. By the 1860s, New York's ready-to-wear manufacturers were well established. Based on an influx of German and Austrian Jewish refugees, the industry was notorious for 'sweating' but highly successful because it was geared to producing 'the right clothes at the right price': as a direct result, for the last years of the nineteenth century most of the couture models on which US mass production was based came from Berlin and Vienna – in the 1890s, thriving centres of high fashion. By 1905,

Red, white and blue berets make a patriotic splash in this *Vogue* picture by Horst.

they had lost the battle to be the inspiration for the American industry. The top American stores, Lord & Taylor, B. Altman & Co and Henri Bendel, had switched their allegiance to Paris. The move rankled especially with the Germans – a fact which was to have repercussions in Paris during World War II. The European publishing business, however, was dominated by Germany and Austria much longer, even into World War I. Eighty per cent of the fashion magazines circulating in Paris in 1915, all with French names, were produced in Frankfurt, Vienna or Berlin.

Immediately before World War I Paris was the mecca for well-dressed women worldwide. Equally valuably, it attracted the professional fashion buyers from the great stores in every civilised city on earth. Only those who intended to buy were invited to couture collections. To most women, the inside of a great couturier's salon was a dark and mysterious secret, revealed only to the richest of private customers or the most powerful of store buyers. The press were not admitted. Exclusivity and secrecy were all. The enemy was the fashion pirate; the fear that he would be able to flood the market with cheap and poorly made copies before the top stores could make their copies from the originals for which they had paid dear. The most despised were the 'renters'.

The renters' game was known to the Paris houses. It must be said that some of the less scrupulous sold them models and then turned a blind eye to the damage this did to other customers working at a slower speed.

In those days, as everyone in Paris knew, the element of surprise was crucial to fashion. Those who had it made money; those who lost it did not. How the renter operated was as simple as it was lucrative, but it was extremely damaging to the high-class stores and dressmaking establishments which made up the majority of the business clients for Paris couture. On receiving the consignment of dresses – legally bought, paid for and imported – in New York the renter then invited manufacturers who had not been to Paris to view them for a fee of anything up to $150,000. Having done so – and viewing included sketching, measuring and in some cases borrowing the models – they were at liberty to reproduce them, sell them more cheaply than bona fide manufacturers, and make the profit which came from being first in the field. All that the top stores could offer to cap them and justify a price tag twice as high was the original French material and possibly – but by no means certainly – a higher class of workmanship.

Renting, like any piracy, was lucrative. As late as 1948 it was calculated that a renter who paid an average of 150,000 francs each for twenty-five garments – an investment of 3,750,000 francs – and then showed them in thirty American cities to an average of fifty clients, made 52,500,000 francs – a net profit on his original investment of 46,750,000 francs. Although fashion houses charged an entrance fee in Paris of up to £1,000, which was credited against any purchases, they could hardly compete with such profits. It was a system that could be beaten only by the change of attitude which came with ready-to-wear. Instead of the press being banned in the cause of secrecy, they were welcomed with open arms in the interests of publicity. With clothes featured in newspapers on the day they were shown, the need for renters was removed.

It was not just the North American manufacturing clients who kept Paris couture in business during the Twenties and Thirties. Private customers from all over the world bought regularly from their favourite houses. South Americans were especially valued but the best spenders were – as they always had been – the provincial dressmakers of France and the minor couture houses of Europe, especially those of Belgium and Spain. All were looking for fashion's *je ne sais quoi* which they felt only Paris could provide. Cristobal Balenciaga, who in the Fifties was the most influential couturier in Paris and is today generally acknowledged as the greatest fashion designer of the last fifty years, began his career in his native Spain by buying couture models from France and selling them and his versions made up in his workrooms, exactly on the American system. Cutters-up – as people who bought the rights to make the garments were called – bought everything required from the couturier and his suppliers, even down to the buttons and belts, so that the original could be exactly recreated.

The late Twenties had been a fabulous time for French fashion. The Chambre Syndicale de la Couture Parisienne, the governing body of Paris couture establishments, had done much to put France's major industry on a proper footing. But the Wall Street Crash meant that the Thirties started with a feeling of insecurity. Many Paris fashion houses which had relied too heavily for their existence on the wives of French industrialists and American store buyers were forced to close. It has been estimated that clients dropped by at least a third and even the 'big' houses were feeling the pinch.

In 1931, *The New York Times* registered a 40 per cent drop in French dress imports to the US. It was a situation which never rectified itself. Even though the trade with France gradually built up again over the decade the hiatus had given American designers confidence and, more importantly, American buyers confidence in *them*. For the first time, American dress designers could walk boldly on to the international fashion scene

The American designer Claire McCardell, who used 'non-fashion' fabrics like denim, was the most forward-looking voice in Forties fashion.

without feeling upstaged by the French. World class talents appeared: Claire McCardell, one of the major influences on sportswear fashion in the second half of the century; Hattie Carnegie, whose taste re-educated a whole generation of American women; and Lilly Daché, arguably the best milliner ever to work in America. They and the many other excellent designers to emerge at this time were given enthusiastic support by the US press, including *Vogue* and *Harper's Bazaar*.

American fashion didn't instantly lose its dependence on Paris by gaining this new self-confidence. US fashion magazines still gave generous coverage to the French collections. Women in New York who wished to wear Paris clothes had a choice, depending on their budget. They could buy the original French model; an exact copy, using the same material; a cheaper copy; or a US design 'based' on the Paris original but specifically geared to American taste and fashion sense.

But what America had, uniquely, at this time, were two elements which meant that the US fashion industry had a power not found elsewhere. Seventh Avenue and Hollywood gave American fashion the edge over its competitors. Seventh Avenue is known as the business centre of the US garment business but, in the Thirties, it was much more. It was the cultural hub of the nation's fashion. Every manufacturer of stature located his headquarters there. All the top department stores – whose influence on fashion was immense – were found in and around it. Every exclusive shop and dressmaker's establishment – along with milliners and all the accessory makers – clustered close by. It was the home of the ready-to-wear industry which was destined to lead the world in advanced production techniques and marketing skills.

LEFT AND ABOVE: Adrian's costumes for Garbo in *Queen Christina* were taken up by some Paris couturiers, especially Schiaparelli.

But that was in the future. The prevailing influence in the Thirties was Hollywood. It created its own fashion designers, many of whom, like Adrian, would eventually leave the studios and set up as couturiers enjoying a world reputation. As early as 1933 it was apparent that a film could not only create fashion fads but also influence even Paris. In that year Adrian created a magnificently rich series of costumes for Greta Garbo in *Queen Christina*, his influence being the gold braid and rigorous tailoring of the nineteenth-century Prussian cavalry. The mood was immediately taken up in Paris. Designers used his frogged velvet and sable dresses as the basis for a rich evening look which was considered the height of luxury. Forty years later it was revisited by Yves Saint Laurent for his Ballets Russes collection in 1976, which is seen as one of the highlights of twentieth-century high fashion. The thread of fashion stretches far.

There were other far-reaching effects from Adrian's film work. The slinky scarlet bugle-bead evening dress made for Joan Crawford in her 1937 film *The Bride Wore Red* spawned a million copies

Claire McCardell's elegantly understated clothes looked superb on Lauren Bacall, who had the confidence to know that less is more when aiming for sophistication.

Joan Crawford's scarlet bugle-bead evening dress in *The Bride Wore Red* was the equal of anything to be seen in Paris and was copied at all levels of the fashion industry.

but, in fact, Adrian's apotheosis as a fashion influence had come as early as 1932 with his famous padded shoulders for Crawford in *Letty Lynton*. It was a fashion taken up by the designer Elsa Schiaparelli for her military look, which was to be a prevailing style during the war, fitting, as it did, with the desire felt by many women to wear clothes that were cut along the lines of the uniforms worn by the men – and, indeed, women – at the front. But whether it would have happened if Adrian hadn't created the mood on which Schiaparelli capitalised is one of the unanswerable questions of twentieth-century fashion which begs the even bigger one: was the wartime look inspired not by a Paris couturier but by a Hollywood studio designer? If so, the fashion influence of Hollywood must be acknowledged as even greater than already conceded.

It was not just Schiaparelli who looked west. Every couturier in Paris had his eyes – and even his sights – set on Hollywood; not always successfully. Lanvin, Lelong, Patou, Poiret, Chanel, Worth: the list of those lured into designing film costume was long, the results largely

438

In 1943 *Vogue* used actresses Penelope Dudley-Ward (left) and Judy Campbell (below) to prove that 'Life Goes On' and elegance could be attained with a little effort.

undistinguished. The attraction of working in Hollywood was the same for couturiers as for actors: film was the consummate art form of exposure. Fame was the spur to a creative class aware of the commercial advantages of marrying an exclusive image and an internationally famous name. Perfume sales had proved that those unable to afford the clothes were happy to buy into the legend on a cheaper level. It was the first stirring of a movement which would culminate in the Eighties paradox of the multi-millionaire dress designers whose wealth came almost entirely from sales of items other than clothes.

By the end of the Thirties, Hollywood had made America such a leader of casual, sporting style that its fashions were becoming desirable worldwide. America's ready-to-wear industry was more sophisticated in fit and sizing than any equivalent in Europe or Britain. Manufacturers were so far ahead in production techniques that US clothing was often able to be sold cheaper than local creations. An article in *Fashion Group Quarterly* of autumn 1939, published in London, pointed out that West End stores were doing a brisk trade with 'breath-takingly' smart housecoats in American cotton at only 4s 11d each, adding rather bitterly that, thanks to American know-how and fashion nous, 'style is now obtainable even in chain stores at any price up to 5s'. The writer knew why. 'With a tariff of twenty per cent and a cotton industry in a pretty bad patch, it is still worthwhile London stores featuring American cotton...piece-goods ordered by the making up trade can be delivered quicker from America than Lancashire...'

Britain couldn't fight back on that level. Its weapon was couture, not cheaper ready-to-wear. Even before the Fall of Paris in 1940, its couturiers had joined battle with the French, not in the hope of ousting them but in the belief that they had something uniquely British which Americans wanted. The New York World Fair of 1939 had made Americans internationally minded and this was an added incentive. At the beginning of August 1939, Hardy Amies at Lachasse had twelve out of fifty models chosen by American manufacturers to be reproduced in the States. It might not seem a very impressive achievement to modern eyes, but in fact it was good trading and, despite the growing rumours of imminent hostilities, promised well for London's future prospects.

War came less than a month later, throwing London fashion into disarray and the government's export policy into confusion. *Women's Wear Daily* of September 1939 reported that 'seventeen days from the outbreak of war, the London fashion trade

is beginning to sort itself out and assume something like normality again.' Despite working with a staff reduced from 400 to 200, Hartnell was doing a good trade in dinner frocks and tailored clothes but reported a complete lack of interest in frills and full skirts. Hardy Amies, in the army as private No. 7686146, had closed Lachasse temporarily and its premises in Farm Street, Mayfair, were being used as an ARP rest centre. Other houses were closed or working on a dramatically reduced level. The Phoney War was about to begin.

Norman Hartnell, By Appointment Dressmaker to the Queen, checking a dress against his original sketch.

Known in France as the *drôle de guerre*, it had much the same effect on the couture houses there as in London. With heavy bombardments expected, most employees were evacuated from Paris. Those who were left walked aimlessly around carrying what Schiaparelli dismissed as their 'useless' gas masks. After a while she persuaded her workers to return so that she might reopen her house – a lead followed by most others, although working on a much smaller scale. Demand for haute couture had almost disappeared, as tourists dashed to leave the country before it was too late. Private customers, finding it more expedient to buy ready-to-wear because the 'big occasion' glamour had gone from Paris life, (although theatres, closed at the outset of war, had reopened) left dresses unfinished and unclaimed on the hands of the couturiers.

Print dresses, the Englishwoman's favourite, with hat and gloves – appropriate for most social events in the Forties' day.

But it was still possible to feel optimistic. In January 1940, a report in *Vogue* pinpointed the two sides of the situation: 'Paris gradually grows more normal,' it wrote. 'When you go to be fitted at Molyneux he complains that he has so many fittings he'll never get through the day... just a few weeks ago, he feared he might never make another jacket.'

This was only half the story. Molyneux seemed busy because he had fewer staff. He was known for his elegant daywear and so was much less hit by the change in French social life than other houses whose speciality was glamorous evening wear – still the staple for those who came to Paris to buy. Even so, he showed a collection of only thirty models where, previously, he had shown over a hundred. But, at least, in response to government encouragement, the shows took place. Three months earlier that would have seemed an impossibility.

June 1940 changed everything. Paris fell and German tanks swerved their way up the Champs Elysées. As jackboots resounded in the elegant halls of fashion, it seemed that Hitler had done what nobody else could – opened up a chink which other fashion capitals would try to widen. There was a real feeling of concern in America. Where would the inspiration for fashion now be found?

There was a feeling of hope in London, despite the horrors of the Blitz. Could Mayfair take the lead?

Above all, there was a sense of betrayal. To many, Paris seemed to have come to its knees too easily. As a prominent member of the New York fashion establishment put it, 'I must teach my children not to hate France...that this which we see and are still to see is not the true France, only a mask of fear and hate and shame.' He was reacting to rumours that the couture houses – by no means alone – were collaborating with the Nazis, to the extent of accepting their anti-Semitic purges and entertaining them in their houses. The facts are grim enough. Of 250,000 French citizens deported during the Occupation, over 100,000 were Jewish. By 1945, at least 625,000 French-men had been shipped to Germany as forced labour.

For the Germans, taking Paris was a major coup of the war. As German officers and men flooded into the city, they were keen to find the glamour, sauciness and *joie de vivre* which had made it a byword for hedonism. Above all – and at the highest level – they were keen to know the couture which, to people all over the world, *was* Paris. German officers went on a wild spending spree, snapping up luxury goods, such as silk stockings, fine perfumes, handbags and shoes, to send back to their women. Although many couture houses refused to deal with them, others did and were immediately dubbed 'collaborators' – soon to become one of the most loathed words in the language. Others, such as Lanvin, which had opened branches in Cannes in the Thirties when the demand for luxury goods reached a high point in the South of France, traded from there, doing good business with wealthy refugees.

The democracy of fashion was immediately menaced. One of the first acts of the Nazi conquerors was to break into the offices of the Chambre Syndicale and seize all documents, including those dealing with the export trade and the dressmaking schools. Their plan seemed simple but was totally unworkable. Thinking, perhaps, of the days when America briefly looked to Germany and Austria for fashion inspiration, they intended to move a sizeable portion of the haute couture industry to Berlin and Vienna to become a focus and figurehead of the German fashion industry and to spearhead a new export trade for the German Reich.

The plans were devastating to French ears. Dressmaking schools, staffed by French couture workers, were to be opened in both cities. Although Paris houses would be permitted to continue operating on a very limited scale, they would not be allowed the monopoly of couture. German officials were unmoved when it was pointed out that to train a first-class couture worker took seven years and the average couture garment required at least 120 hours' work to complete. They felt sure that their people could cope as well as the French.

These were dark and dangerous days for Paris fashion, filled with suspicions, fears and mistrust. But out of the darkness appeared a champion. Lucien Lelong, born in Paris on 11 October 1889, was a true son of the city. In World War I, he had been one of the first seven Frenchmen to be awarded the Croix de Guerre, but was severely injured in 1917. Although he had no love of Germans, he knew when Paris collapsed that, as President of the Chambre Syndicale – a post he had held since 1937 – he must negotiate with them to save the industry. Of his determination not to be beaten there was already evidence.

After war had been declared, the mid-season showings in Paris had failed to attract any American buyers. Lelong personally invited 150 New

A wedding dress drawn by Maureen Wells, who worked for Peter Russell, realising his ideas in sketches to show to clients.

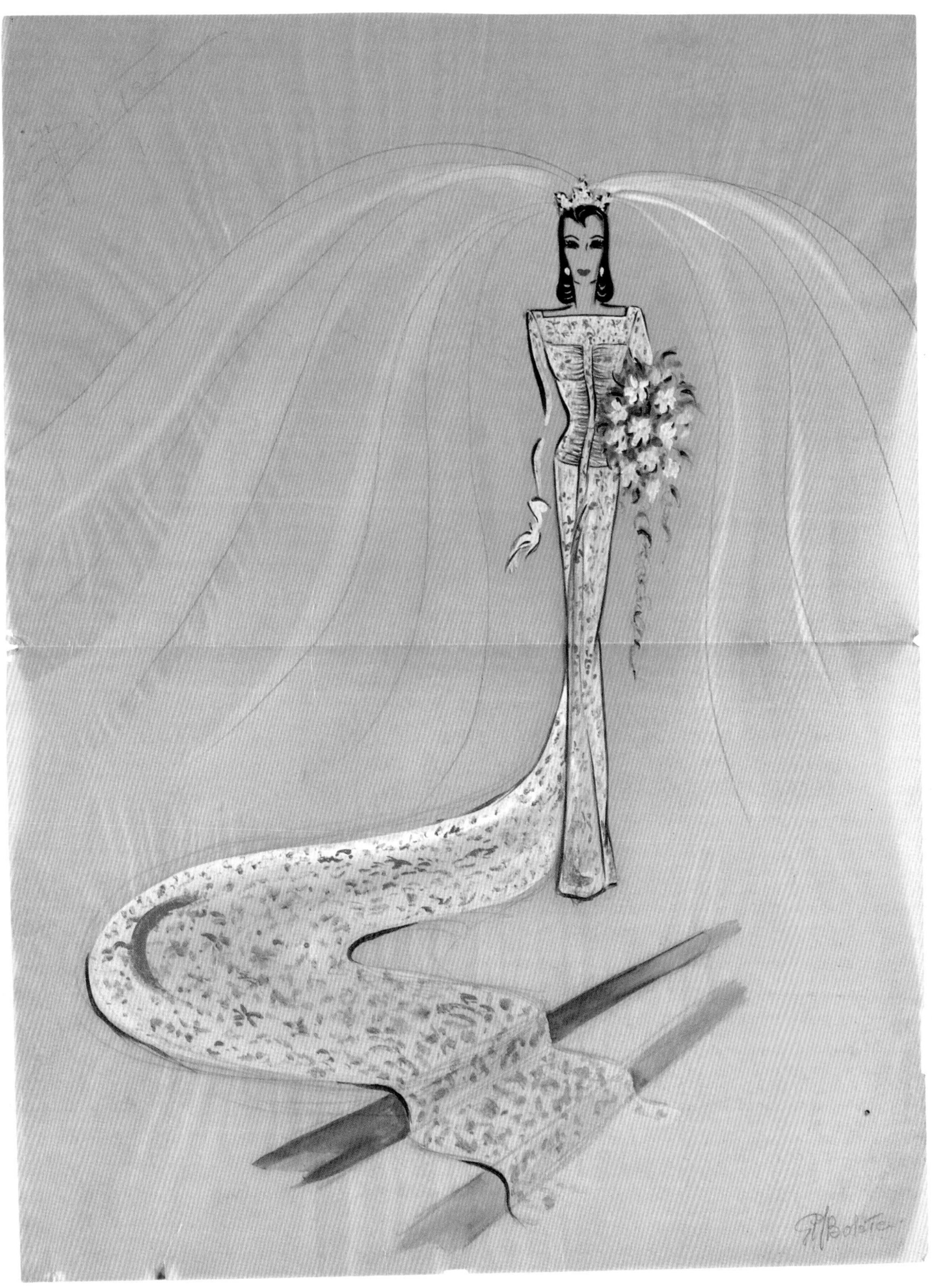

York buyers for the January 1940 collections, arranging for their boat to land in Italy and then organising a special train to take them to Paris where he persuaded the French Ministries of Information and Commerce to host a reception for them – a 'first' since copied worldwide. Such a man was clearly not going to give in without a fight.

Lucien Lelong, President of the Chambre Syndicale, whose diplomatic efforts saved French couture.

On the most practical of levels, the situation in Paris was grim. To aid their own war effort, the German authorities confiscated 80 per cent of French-made fabrics. The government of Marshal Pétain took 17 per cent to clothe soldiers, police and officials, leaving 3 per cent of production to dress the whole of France. In the many discussions Lelong had with the Germans – over the four years of the Occupation there were fourteen official high-level conferences and innumerable meetings, recorded and not recorded, between the protagonists – he slowly began to make them realise the impracticality of their plan. Knowing that the greatness of French couture relied on intangibles, he persuaded the Germans that without the French cultural tradition which Paris alone could give, not only would it simply not survive, but without its inspiration, Berlin and Viennese fashion could also be menaced.

The Germans were in a cleft stick. Frequently, they threatened to crush Paris couture if Lelong refused to move it to Berlin. They introduced punitive regulations: in 1941, they produced clothing ration cards, each worth 100 points. This had an immediate and adverse affect on couture. Even a modest jacket containing a minimum amount of wool swallowed up forty points. In fact, it seemed that all the fashion houses would be forced to close. After lengthy discussions, Lelong persuaded the Germans to allow twelve of them to remain open. The Nazis agreed because they knew that there was plenty of black market money in France, keen to be spent quickly and flamboyantly. The Germans themselves were buying Paris clothes. Fashion was an excellent source of tax revenue which the Reich did not wish to lose. As Lelong said, 'Before the war, it was estimated that one couture dress exported paid for ten tons of imported coal, and a litre of perfume exported permitted two tons of gasoline to be imported.' Armed with these arguments to show that couture, far from being effete and degenerate, was a proven earner of revenue, Lelong went to Berlin in November 1940 to put his case.

A compromise was reached. Couture customers were allowed to exchange a portion of their clothing ration cards for 'couture creation' cards which could be used only for couture garments at an agreed number of houses. But there was an anxious moment when the authorities found out that, instead of the agreed twelve, there were ninety-two fashion houses still functioning in Paris. They were furious at the defiance but Lelong managed to defuse the situation so successfully that they agreed to sixty being kept open.

This was a major victory, but Lelong and his colleagues continued to have their difficulties. There were still suspicions, terror and total unpredictability under German rule. The conquerors showed their unhappiness and frustration at what they saw as the defiance of the couture industry by issuing edicts making impossible demands. At one point, they announced that 80 per cent of the workers in some couture houses were to be drafted into industries more clearly linked to the German war effort. Other houses were told they would lose only 10 per cent of their force. The decision was totally arbitrary. Lelong again argued and had the number reduced to a 5 per cent quota for all houses. It has been estimated that less than 3 per cent of the fashion work force was actually affected in the end. It was really a war of nerves, not practicality, in which the Germans were indulging. By the end of the Occupation, Lelong had saved 97 per cent of the couture industry and had rescued at least 112,000 workers from the threat of choosing between compulsory unemployment and a life of forced labour in the German war industries.

Throughout the Occupation, the survival of the couture industry was always touch and go. In the end, Lelong won not on ideology but on straightforward economic common sense. For his own ends, he fostered the illusion that Paris and Berlin were working together for mutual benefit. In fact, he was actively working against Germany behind the scenes. When the Germans closed Madame Gres' house, the Chambre Syndicale secretly paid her laid-off workers. When – in an attempt to bring the wayward industry under control – the Germans froze all couture wages, the Chambre produced funds for the couture houses to pay bonuses in order to keep wages up to the level of inflation. It was all part of Lelong's determination that the French couture would not be suppressed.

To keep it vibrant under the Nazis, he set up a 'Committee of Appreciation' which selected anonymously submitted models in order to decide which houses were worthy of support. He was especially keen to encourage young ones, as they were obviously the future for couture. In 1942, to show the world that French couture still existed as *French* couture, he arranged a fashion show in Lyons which attracted 300 buyers from Africa, Switzerland, Spain, Italy and Portugal. It was a convincing but silent argument to counter

A Lucien Lelong day dress demonstrating how even the top couturiers in Paris were having to economise on materials by 1943.

A hat by Rose Descat, with the current feeling for height, photographed by Lee Miller in the milliner's salon in 1944.

the Nazi demands and fitted well with a survey, also made in 1942, which revealed that 50,000 French firms still functioning in the couture, lingerie, millinery, men's tailoring and shirt-making industries were doing an annual business of just under 4 billion francs.

Away from the negotiation tables of haute couture, the women of Paris were being more openly defiant to their occupiers. In order to demonstrate their contempt for what they saw as the lumpen Hun soldiery, the female members of which they nicknamed *soeurs grises* – grey sisters – they dressed as gaily as they possibly could. As the couturier Mad Carpentier told American listeners in a broadcast after the Liberation of Paris, 'They, who liked to think themselves our conquerors, must never be able to pity us... I know what it costs to be able to look the Boche in the face and think, "You have taken everything from us and yet we manage to look as if we have everything."'

In fact, they had almost nothing but their Gallic spirit. Everything was rationed but, even then, there was virtually nothing in the shops. The black market flourished on a scale and with an openness which would have appalled the English and Americans, but it was excused as being the only way to obtain anything. There was a thriving clandestine market for coupons. Amazingly, women managed to keep themselves looking presentable. Whereas in England women's clothes took on a military look with masculine, square shoulders and mannish proportions, the women of France wanted their dress to demonstrate to the Germans that no amount of restriction and coercion could kill their spirit as women.

Carmel Benito, who worked at Reboux, one of the most famous milliners in Paris, has pinpointed the feeling of the time:

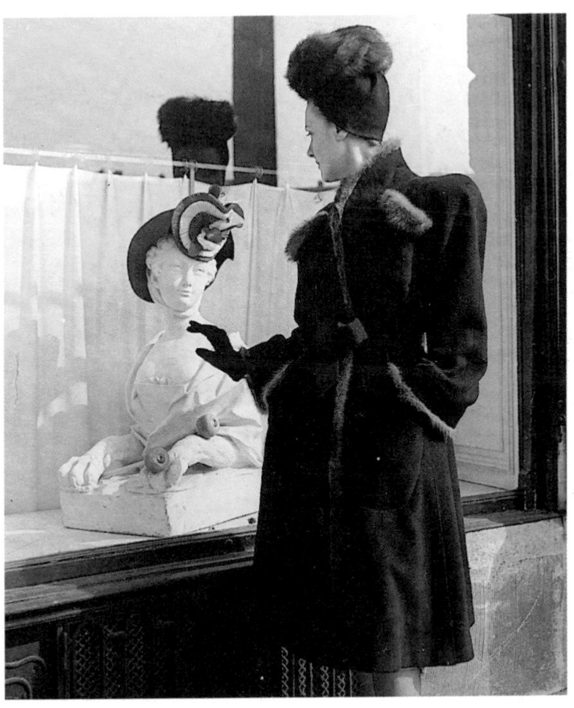

Paris was famous for its extravagant and fanciful millinery, a defiant gesture against the Germans.

'We wore large hats to raise our spirits. Felt gave out, so we made them of chiffon. Chiffon was no more. All right, take straw. No more straw? Very well, braided paper... hats have been a sort of contest between French imagination and German regulation ... We were prepared to do without food, light, soap, servants; we were prepared to choke in overcrowded Metros and go everywhere else on foot: but we wouldn't look shabby and worn out. After all, we were Parisiennes...We didn't get excited about ladders either, as there were no stockings to be found. It took a long time

painting our legs brown...we wore dirndls made of curtains...there was nothing to eat but bread, greyer than ever after four years.'

When, in 1944, Paris was regained, Lee Miller, the photographer and journalist, was one of the first people to arrive in the city with the liberating US forces. Her impressions were printed in *Vogue*. 'The French concept of civilised life has been maintained,' she wrote. 'But at a heavy price.' She pointed out that, in contrast to London, the women of Paris thought it was an act of patriotism to flaunt regulations by dressing as exuberantly and extravagantly as imagination and inspiration could contrive, because any saving of material could only benefit the Germans: 'If three yards were specified for a dress, they found fifteen for a skirt alone.' But she was also perceptive enough to know that the 'amplitude of material was used to offset undernourished figures'. Those French who had refused to collaborate with their oppressors had virtually starved during the Occupation. But the Liberation day crowds showed little sign of the privations they had suffered. As Miller reported, 'Everywhere in the streets were the dazzling girls... their silhouette was very queer and fascinating... after utility and austerity England. Full floating skirts, tiny waistlines. They were top-heavy with built-up Pompadour front hair-dos and waving tresses' – a style known as the Cadogan in France – 'weighted to the ground with clumsy, fancy thick-soled wedge shoes. The entire gait of the French woman has changed with her footwear. Instead of the bouncing buttock and mincing steps of "pre-war", there is a hot-foot, long stride...'

A romantic rose hat worn with a severely chic town suit, photographed by Lee Miller shortly after the Liberation of Paris.

Paris fashion – cut off from the world – had taken its own route. Michel de Brunhoff, editor of French *Vogue*, explained why the magazine had ceased publication after the Occupation: 'There was no honourable way under the Germans.' He had refused to budge, despite their insistence, although he had clandestinely produced Fashion Albums without German knowledge or permission. He agreed with Miller's assessment of the dress codes of Paris: 'By the third winter, the Nazis could be taunted. The big wooden shoes of necessity became fancy creations instead of farmyard utility. Hats soared to balance the silhouette.' Outrageous headgear, much of it too bizarre to be called millinery, was an especially effective goad. The Germans knew that they were being teased by these large, flamboyant concoctions, but could not control them. When they complained – to Lelong among others – they were met with a Gallic shrug and the reply that it was the fashion – although, as an act of expediency, the couture houses countered the movement on the streets by showing small hats. The women who defiantly cycled around Paris took no notice and their hats became even wilder. Cellophane, newspapers, scraps of pre-war material – everything was possible. They were the talk of Paris. Christian Dior thought they looked like 'huge pouffes that denied both the period's woes and plain common sense'. They reminded the playwright Jean Cocteau of puff pastries and the novelist Colette of rum babas.

There was more to it than fun. Those crazy hats were the outward sign of something rather desperate in French fashion. London and New York were amazed in autumn 1944 when pictures of the first post-Liberation collections appeared in newspapers and magazines. The coupon-controlled British were offended by what they saw as an insult to their own parlous condition in the gaiety and wanton spirit of the amount of material the French used. There was so much annoyance that in December of that year Lucien Lelong – realising that a political rift had been created –

M V

sent a message to both countries, via *Vogue:* 'It was only after the Autumn Collections were shown that I received copies of English and American dress restrictions and I now understand why certain journalists found the Paris Collections exaggerated... It must be remembered that, although these Collections were finished whilst we were once more officially at war, they were conceived during the excitement of the few days preceding and following the Liberation.'

In fact, the extravagance which had so annoyed France's allies was largely illusory. The Chambre Syndicale imposed rules on the couturiers. The 150 models traditionally shown were cut to a maximum of forty. Not more than half the models could be in woollen fabrics and even those were to contain no more than 30 per cent of actual wool. The amount of material in each model was strictly controlled – no more than 3½ yards for a dress, four for a suit and four and two thirds for a coat, but the skills of the couturier could often make three yards look like six by cunning use of a bias cut, simulated pleats, narrow skirts with full bodices and wide skirts with tight ones. After all, this sort of legerdemain was what the customers had always paid Paris couturiers for – although now the prices were also controlled, running from 8,000 to 15,000 francs. Midinettes – the girls who worked in the couture houses and milliners' – were paid 600 francs per month. With chronic petrol shortages and a crowded, unreliable Metro system, many walked for miles across Paris to spend a day working without gas or electricity and no heating, which meant that they couldn't even iron.

The only fuel in Paris belonged to the Allied forces, so it was both chic and practical to cycle everywhere, especially when showing off the newest wedge heels.

Difficulties notwithstanding, the German

Occupation undoubtedly had a deep and lasting effect on Paris couture. Apart from Lelong's efforts it is easy to see the period as a shameful one. The fashion industry does not come out of it with entirely clean hands. Collaboration there was – and with it betrayals and dishonesties. Chanel, who lived with a high-ranking German officer, was not the only transgressor. But the problem went deeper. During the Occupation France lost vital ground in that it became apparent that the fashion industry of the world did not require a lead from French couture and, in fact, could move more quickly without it.

The four years during which Paris ceased to dominate world fashion were crucially wounding to couture. Further, they allowed other cities to gain credibility for their creativity. The present fashion system, in which couture is largely irrelevant and Paris is one of several fashion capitals – neither necessarily more influential nor richer – would have been inconceivable in the Forties, but it was in those years that the change of attitude occurred. The couture shows of 1944 amazed the world not with their beauty and glamour but because of their old-fashioned bourgeois appearance.

Four years of Occupation had made Paris provincial and, although it recovered and cast off its dowdiness, a self-indulgence had crept in which was not to go away. The vigour, energy and drive vital to fashion creativity had crossed the Atlantic.

The French couturiers had been encouraged in complacency by one thing: they did not have to compete in the marketplace. Germany, Spain and the Axis countries bought all of the limited number of clothes they could produce.

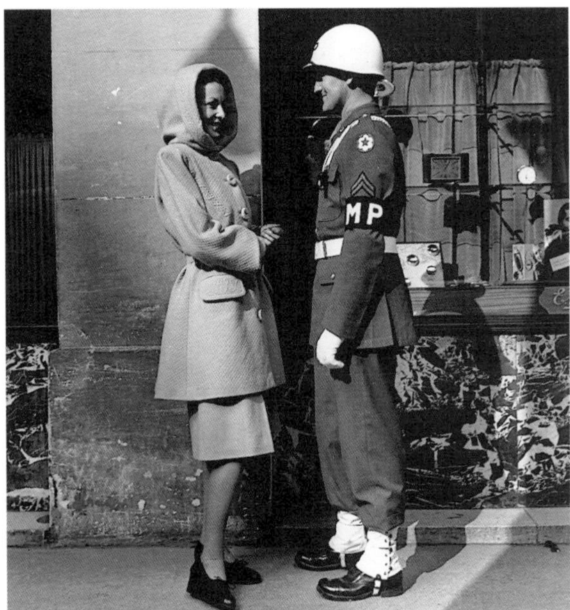

Paris fashion was given the thumbs up by the liberating US army, eager to see glamour again.

War had been quite different for the English couturiers. In March 1939 *Women's Wear Daily* reported that the London collections had started badly, with only one American model buyer in town, which the newspaper put down as much to the New York World Fair as to any worries over peace: 'Activities reached their peak when three New York manufacturers turned up in Bruton Street on the same day, then tailed off.' It was not just Lucien Lelong who was having trouble attracting the American buyers immediately before the war. But, for all their restrictions and difficulties, once war came the London couturiers had the great advantage over those in Paris: England was free and could carry on trade across the Atlantic when France could not.

After the capture of Paris, London's efforts were concentrated on taking the fashion lead. The government, desperate to earn dollars, was happy to lend support, but the couturiers realised that the task would not be easy. Not only was New York strong enough to be self-sufficient, it had been strengthened further by the arrival of Mainbocher and Schiaparelli from France. England had also been helped: by the return to London of Edward Molyneux. His importance as a rallying point for the efforts of British couture was immense because he was so well known in New York.

Harper's Bazaar justifiably sang his praises in January 1941, pointing out how he was using his stature to interest the American buyers in London clothes. The figures resulting from his involvement were impressive. As the magazine explained, 'The minimum number of models a good American import house is buying over the year is forty-five. At a conservative estimate, American houses would make twenty-five repeats of each model. These repeats would require, on an average, £15 worth of English material, including embroidery, belts, buttons etc. The nett total, therefore, ordered by one house, which included the price paid for the forty-five original models, would be £19,125. As there are about twenty houses ordering on this scale, the total value of exports going from England to North America in one year is £382,500. In addition many smaller houses ordering two or three models a season...bring the export total to £500,000.'

Above all, it was Molyneux the North Americans wanted, as the cables received made clear: from San Francisco stores: 'Desperate for Molyneux'; 'Thrilled and excited to have Molyneux clothes'. From New York: 'Clothes divine'; 'Delighted'; 'Perfect – Congratulations'. Chicago: 'A beautiful collection. I think it marvellous that you continue to carry on'. Molyneux's appeal was simple. As the link with Paris, and the only couturier who had worked in that city to continue working, he gave American buyers confidence that the ideas they were buying would have French chic, although made in London. That is why he was such a vital figurehead. In 1946 *Vogue* reported that Molyneux's war effort had raised his business to a turnover of $3m, 'all of which was put at the disposal of the British Government to buy munitions'. Clearly, without him, although Amies at Lachasse, Morton and Stiebel were admired, London would not have been so well regarded by US manufacturers and store buyers.

After all, American designers may have been prepared to bend a knee in the direction of Paris, but they felt in no way inferior to London. And they were right. American fashion was catering for a population much better educated in the nuances of fashion

The Liberation shoe in pigskin and suede was created by Di Mauro in 1944 to honour the Allies.

than the British – and with considerably more spending power. The women of America, like its designers, had been educated in style during the Twenties and the Thirties and had evolved an approach as practical and sporty as it was fashionable. Above all, American fashion was modern – and extremely accomplished. Adrian was a couturier the equal of most in Europe. Norman Norell's clothes could have passed muster if shown in Paris. Pauline Trigère had been born and trained there. Valentina, born in Russia, had lived in Paris and was a friend of Leon Bakst. Mainbocher, who had originally been a fashion artist for *Harper's Bazaar* and later fashion editor of French *Vogue* before becoming a couturier, was an international figure. The sophistication and knowledge to make New York the fashion capital were not lacking. Neither were the skills. Although not in the same league as Paris, American garment workers had a European sensibility – nearly all were refugees.

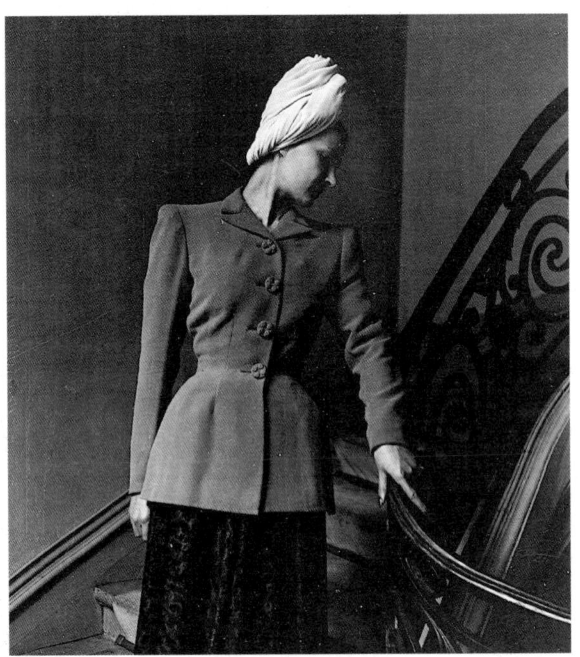

A chic hat was an essential part of any formal outfit in 1944 (above), just as it had been in 1939 (right) – and so were diamonds and furs, if you still possessed them.

Out of the shadow of Paris, no longer required to rely on French fabric and colour sense, they were free to create a truly indigenous fashion look which, because of the glamour America had in the eyes of the world, would attract foreign as well as American customers. Not that American fashion was free of all restraints. The L. 85 restrictions were imposed in 1943 to limit the use of materials deemed necessary for the war effort but, unlike rationing in Britain, they were aimed primarily at manufacturers. In fact, the only item of clothing requiring ration tickets in America was shoes. As in Britain, leather was too vital to the war effort to allow it to be squandered unnecessarily. Contrary to popular British belief, American women did not have unlimited supplies of nylon stockings. The demand for nylon to make parachutes took all that could be produced. Even rayon stockings were hard to come by, as most of its production was also taken up by the war effort.

As in Europe, any material using wool affected the war effort, and the US Government's War Production Board ruled that dresses were not allowed to be wider than 72 inches around the hem. This, along with suit jackets limited to 25 inches in length and trousers narrowing to 14 inches, created a meagre silhouette which respected fabric shortages and was so similar to the one imposed by British austerity rules that it made the fashion of the two countries remarkably coherent – an obvious advantage for dollar-strapped British couturiers hoping to sell in the US. It also explains the puritanical reaction of both countries to the fashion

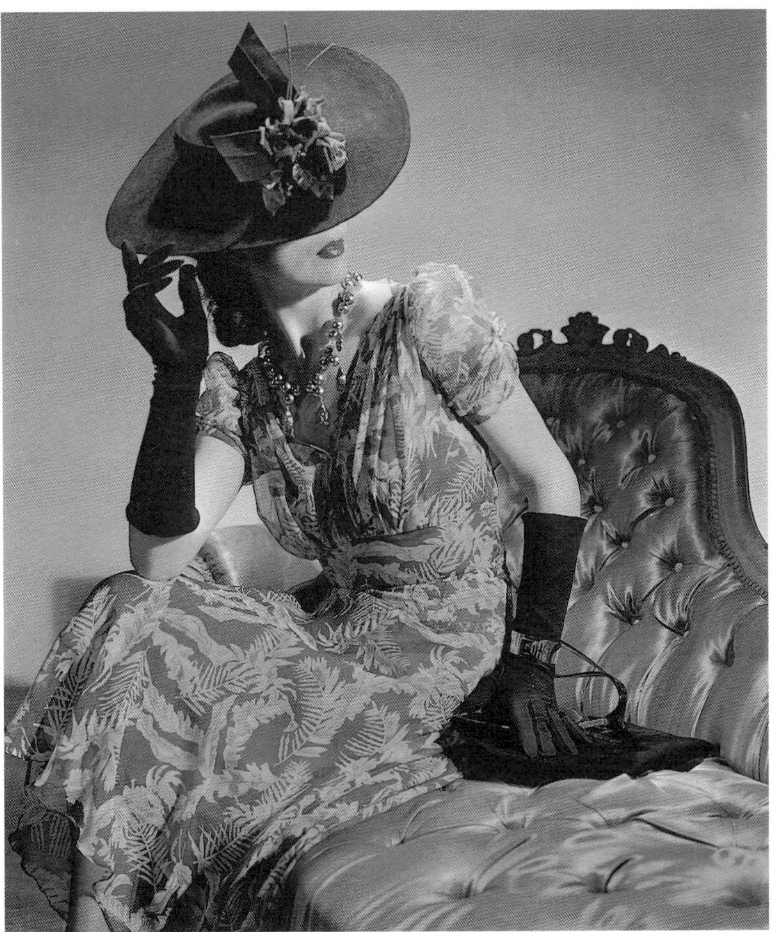

The softly romantic look of chiffon worn with a picture hat was still the ideal of many couturiers.

mood of Paris, revealed after the Liberation. The narrow silhouette was such a standard feature of daytime fashion on both sides of the Atlantic that the billowing Paris styles shocked eyes which had barely seen them since the late Thirties. For the first time in 100 years, Paris had been upstaged. Its clothes looked quaintly out of touch with the tenor of the times to women used to a more radical and simplified fashion approach.

Austerity fashion had been so assiduously promoted by the British Government that it was hard for women to imagine anything else. Even the Queen adhered to the rules and if an impressive dress was required, Hartnell, forced to obey the injunction against the use of embroidery, had to hand-paint any decoration on to the fabric. In his own words, he also 'retinted and rearranged' Her Majesty's pre-war gowns. The tightest restrictions did not apply to garments intended for export. There seemed to be a real possibility of British style capturing an up-market corner of the American fashion scene. There was no lack of enthusiasm for the idea among British couturiers, who started their attack long before the introduction of L. 85, although government officials were less easily convinced.

The *Sunday Referee* in August 1941 reported that the Board of Trade, after a tug of war with the army, had obtained temporary leave for Victor Stiebel (working on camouflage) and Hardy Amies (in Intelligence) to design a collection specifically for the American market. Considering how desperately dollars were needed, it was no great triumph: Stiebel was released for seven days and Amies was granted a few afternoons off. Along with other couturiers, they were to create 300 models to be flown over to New York by Clipper.

A month later, the *News Chronicle*, reporting that the enterprise had been indefinitely postponed, quoted the Board of Trade as saying 'a trade promotion effort in this direction would be untimely at the moment. It is realised that diversion of women's labour from the textile industries to other departments of munitions production must be accelerated...'

There followed a period of confusion over the government's export policy. An announcement by the Department of Overseas Trade, listing 'traditional UK exports to the US' – raw wool, woollen goods and cotton – included some apparel, which the couturiers took as meaning they could sell clothes to America if they had the opportunity. Delivery dates were so unpredictable that Molyneux refused to show in London for fear that copyists might beat him to it and get into America with his designs before he could. His lead was quickly followed. The *Evening Standard* reported that a non-austerity fashion parade held secretly in London had resulted in orders from the United States, Canada, Egypt, Australia, Sweden, Switzerland and Iran – at high prices.

But it was in North and South America that government and couturiers saw the possibility of the richest pickings. In 1940, the Mantle and Costume Export Group was formed under the aegis of the Board of Trade. Its New York show prompted *Harper's Bazaar* to speculate, 'Shall we see the Statue of Liberty warmly clothed this winter in British woollens?' It was a hope taken up by Harcourt Johnson of the Department of Overseas Trade, in an open letter to the British textile industry, in which he pointed out:

> 'British fabrics have led the world in quality since the wool trade was first established in England. British pioneer work in cotton has also displayed a skill and adaptability that still characterise the United Kingdom textile industries and has led to the introduction in recent times by British textile experts of rayons in qualities and styles that have created a modern fashion appeal and contributed to the prosperity of our export trade in textile manufactures.
>
> 'The old-established fabrics, linens and silks, have also upheld their great reputation for quality and design, and like the other branches of the textile industry they are utilising fully the services of their research institutions and the newly formed Export Groups to maintain their leading position in the world's markets.
>
> 'The outbreak of the second Great War and the resultant eclipse of Paris and Vienna as centres of women's fashions have created a gap that the United Kingdom textile industries have been quick to appreciate,

Mainbocher was one of New York's most talented designers. Having lived and worked in Paris for many years, he understood how to marry European and American elegance.

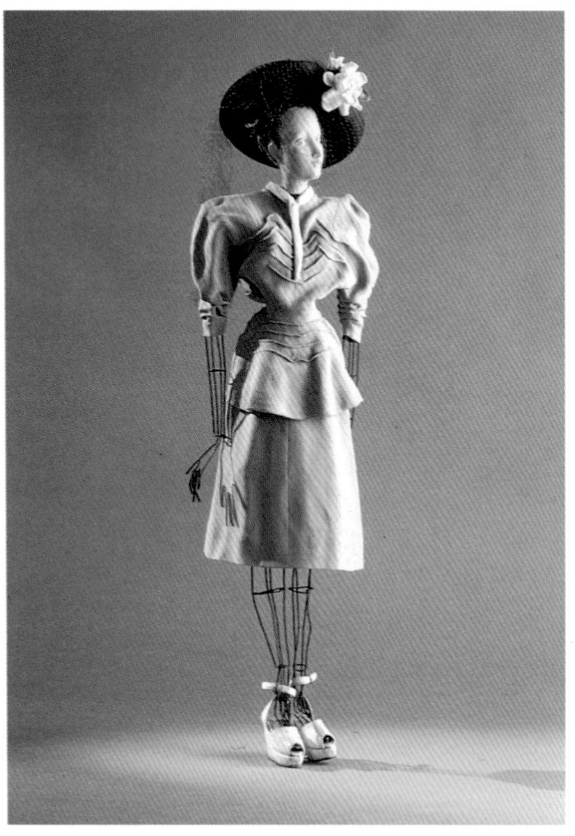

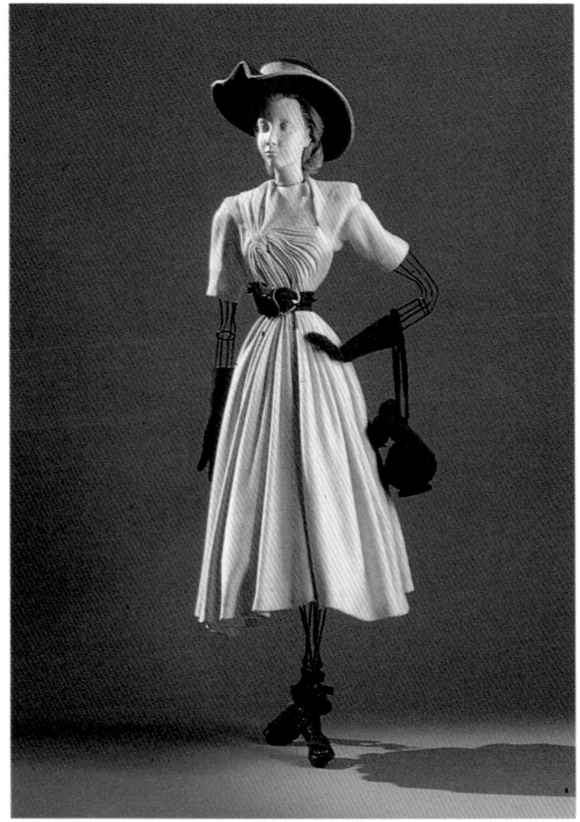

ABOVE: Mannequins by couturiers Lafaurie (left) and Dormay (right), created for the Théâtre de la Mode, in 1945.

and every effort is being put forward to create a centre of women's fashion in Great Britain comparable with the pre-eminent position of London in the world of men's wear.'

1941 was the year of the great putsch. In March it was the South American market that was in the sights. A fashion mission was sent to Rio de Janeiro, Sao Paolo, Buenos Aires and Montevideo, encouraged by a message from the Export Council pointing out that the South American Fashion show would have 'the double effect of increasing export opportunities for fashion clothes...and bringing in currency for many things we need in fighting this war to a victorious conclusion.' Efforts and ingenuity were brought to bear in May, when a motor caravan toured North American women's universities to show British fashions. In June the British Women's Fashion Trade Export Group had a major exhibition touring US and Canadian cities, consisting of 200 garments, worn by twelve American models and nine English models just back from Brazil. The New York show had a splendidly kitsch finale with the nine British girls leading a British bulldog with 'We Can Take It' on his collar to the accompaniment of a band playing 'There'll Always Be an England'. By 1943 things were less exuberant. The highlight of the year was an exhibition in October of figurines representing the countries of South America, dressed by Hartnell in festive costume, the proceeds from which went to the Soldiers', Sailors' and Armies' Families Association.

Was it all this activity which gave the French couturiers the idea for the Théâtre de la Mode, conceived by Monsieur Dautry, President of L'Entraide Française, and Robert Ricci of the fashion house Nina Ricci, as a way of gathering money for the Social Service Fund by using snippets from the floors of high fashion workrooms while garnering publicity for French couture? Regardless of origins, it was a brilliant idea which fulfilled both hopes. The exhibition, held in the Pavillon Marsan in the Louvre in March 1945, attracted 100,000 visitors before being taken to New York, where it was received with equal enthusiasm, having already been seen in London, Leeds, Copenhagen, Stockholm, Barcelona and Vienna.

A maximum of five miniature outifts, made to the most precise standards of couture, was submitted by each of forty-one couture houses in Paris. Shoes, hats, jewellery, gloves were all part of the 'look'. The 237 figures – not dolls but elegant wire sculptures created by Eliane Bonabel – were displayed on thirteen sets, designed by artists of the calibre of Jean Cocteau and Christian Bérard. In London, the exhibition, sponsored by the Continental *Daily Mail*, was opened by the Duchess of Kent and seen by 120,000 visitors. Both light-hearted and serious, it suggested a new direction for Paris fashion, a determination to make up lost ground and a conviction that France alone could supply the imagination, enchantment and glamour, not to mention the skills, which constituted haute couture.

National Savings posters were designed to make the idea of saving not just appealing but also glamorous.

C H A P T E R 5

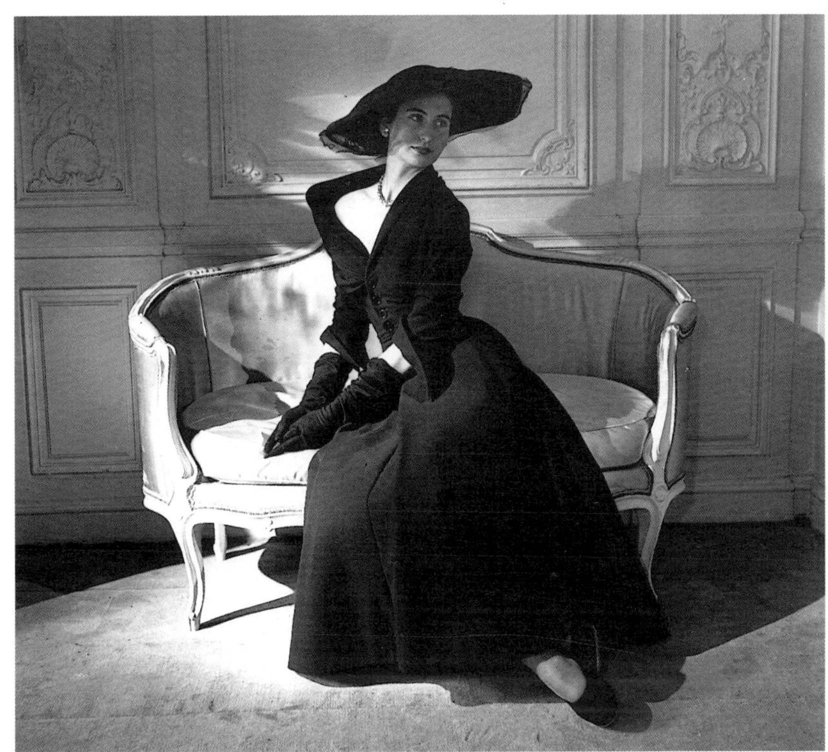

The New Look

The glamour (left) and elegance (above) of Dior's New Look was what women longed for after the war.

French fashion reasserted itself very quickly after Liberation. Not only was the Théâtre de la Mode enchanting thousands around the world, in Paris itself everyone was determined that, as in pre-war fashion, the post-war lead would be French. Even L'Union Nationale des Intellectuels did their bit by co-sponsoring with forty couture houses 'Les Robes Blanches', a show of evening gowns held in the Théâtre des Champs-Elysées on 10 December 1946. In aid of the Maison de la Midinette, the fashion industry's own charity, it was a spectacular affair – although perhaps the most amazing part of it was the involvement of the L'Union Nationale des Intellectuels – such a body could barely exist outside France and only there would it take fashion seriously. The point of the show was not merely newspaper coverage for the French fashion industry, although that was a major consideration after being cut off so completely from the rest of the world during the Occupation that not even *Vogue*, a vital organ of communication for French fashion and read in other countries as almost a semi-official publication, had been published. 'Les Robes Blanches' was more. A carefully conceived and beautifully executed piece of propaganda, its concentration on evening wear was deliberate. Evening gowns, barely seen during the Occupation, carried romantic connotations of the carefree elegance of pre-war life in Paris. They gave hope for the future and raised the spirit of the nation. They were also a slap in the eye to the Germans. Life was starting again: not, this time, for the black-market profiteers and collaborators, but for the true French whose spirit, as this show said so clearly, had not been broken by Nazi oppression.

Every major house, big and small, for which Lelong had battled was represented. All dresses were created in white and the souvenir programme consisted of drawings of examples from the great houses by the top fashion artists in France: Balenciaga, Balmain (who had only recently opened his own house), Jean Desses, Gaston (the house soon to be offered to Christian Dior), Patou or Nina Ricci. The only pre-war house not included was that of Chanel, who had closed in 1939 and spent the war years in retirement. In fact, her behaviour in those years had given rise to so much criticism that to reopen her house in 1946 would have been not just unwise but very dangerous. Always a megalo-maniac, Chanel genuinely believed that anything she willed could be achieved. Her wartime devotion to this delusion has an opera-buffa side to it as well as something much more sinister.

BALENCIAGA

Dior's friends Balenciaga (left) and Balmain (right) both created evening gowns for the Robes Blanches show in 1946.

The accusations of liaising with the Germans

were well-founded. Chanel had a German lover throughout the war. Baron von Dinklage was a Nazi officer and a spy. He was 43, she 56 when they met. He lived with her in the Paris Ritz and she used him and his position to further her own sinister ends. The partners in her perfume business were Jewish. She saw in the Nazis her opportunity to regain total control of her 'name', at no expense, as Jews were technically debarred from doing business in occupied France. She wanted them exposed and run off the premises so that the business could revert to her without her having to pay them any compensation. Her partners frustrated her plan by selling, for the nominal sum of $2,500, their property in France to an 'Aryan', who could legally be the proprietor.

But Chanel's delusions of grandeur did not end there. In 1943, egged on by von Dinklage, she decided to use her privileged position with the British, through her long-term relationship with the Duke of Westminster, to persuade Churchill to negotiate a peace. After much coming and going across Europe, including trips to Madrid and Berlin, her idea came to nothing, but the fact that it occurred at all confirms Chanel's deep involvement with the Nazis.

She was arrested at the time of the Liberation, along with others who had fraternised. Even then, her powerful connections came to the fore. When others were being killed for collaboration much less serious than hers, when women were having their heads shaved and being subjected to public humiliation and scorn, Chanel's friends in high places came to her aid. Her German war connections notwithstanding, Chanel had never quarrelled with her British friends. Her release a few hours after her early morning arrest has been put down to intervention by the Duke of Westminster or even by Churchill. Both are possible. Either way, Chanel avoided the immediate punishments although suffering one much worse. Her behaviour and the fashion world's reaction to it made it impossible for her to reopen her fashion house. Instead, she was forced to keep a low profile. There was a real danger that she could have been tried, or certainly called as a witness, at Nuremberg. Apart from the booming sales of her scent, Chanel No. 5, nobody wanted her name and it had to disappear.

And so had she. Slipped across the border to Switzerland, she lived a life of anonymity, using her vast wealth to silence people and suppress evidence every time her wartime activities looked like resurfacing.

Chanel was not merely a megalomaniac, she was a creative force and the enforced reclusive inactivity which was her lot in Switzerland was surely the greatest punishment that could be meted out to an artist in her prime. Fearful of discovery, she paid out fortunes to have the documents of her wartime schemes burned, but no amount of money could take away her frustration at what was happening in Paris fashion. But she dared not go back. Too many people were still alive, their memories of her behaviour still fresh. For eight years her talent was put on 'hold', until she felt it safe to risk a return. Even then, in 1953, when she reopened her fashion house in rue Cambon, at the age of seventy, her past was not forgotten. The French press savaged her. *Combat* labelled her work 'provincial'; for *L'Aurore* it was 'melancholy'. The English were scarcely more kind. The *Daily Mail* described her show as a flop; the *Daily Express* went further and called it a fiasco. To what extent any of the comments were objective and how much a settling of old scores will never be known. But, had it not been for American enthusiasm, led aggressively by American *Vogue*'s Bettina Ballard, a pre-war friend, the Chanel legend would probably have ended there.

Famed for their silks, Hermès produced a scarf to celebrate the French Resistance, but, due to a shortage of silk and the scarcity of dyes, it was made in wool.

Certainly, it is impossible not to speculate on how fashion might have developed had Chanel lived blamelessly during the war. Would her house have gone on to great heights, like that of Balenciaga – incidentally, the only male couturier for whom Chanel ever expressed admiration – or, missing the tempo of the times, as Schiaparelli and Molyneux were to do, would it have been forced to close again in the early Fifties?

But that was all some way distant. Current problems in France were, like those in Britain – and, indeed, Germany – to do with overcoming chronic shortages and trying to manage within the coupon allocation. French women paid twelve points for a skirt; an artificial silk blouse required six; a cotton sweater nine. A yard of woollen-mix material cost twenty points. Barter was often the only solution. A pre-war woollen dress could be exchanged for a length of woollen material at a reduced points rating and many women took that way out. Even if their dressmakers could do something with the skimpy, poor quality material, there were no zippers or snaps to be had legally. As a chic French woman wrote in a letter after the war, 'It was quite impossible to *dress* and not break the law.'

Things in Germany were no better. The country had been subject to clothes rationing since November 1939. The annual issue of coupons varied between 100 and 150. A wool dress required fifty-six points, a winter coat 100; even a petticoat took twelve. Rather like the British, the Germans were asked to sacrifice a chic appearance for the war effort although, after the Fall of France, the stocking supply – such a drain on morale in the UK – increased considerably.

One of the most frustrating things for women in Britain was the nylon situation. Introduced in America in 1939, over 700,000 pairs were sold on the first day. They became a legend during the war for their scarcity as much as for their sex appeal.

Apart from those made available to US forces personnel, a certain number managed to cross the Atlantic and, by 1946, it was again, a case of 'if you know where to go'. A Swansea matron recalls 'There was a stall in the market at that time run by a Lascar. Nylons day was once a week. He charged £1 per pair, mind you, but the shops – when they ever had them – were selling them for up to 35s. You had to check to see they were a matching pair and not damaged. You never asked where they came from, and you never threw them away. If they laddered you paid to have them invisibly mended.'

'15 denier' became two of the most erotically arousing words in the language. 'Nylons were the biggest temptation since Eve,' a woman in the North East admits. 'You felt out of step if you hadn't got any. After the war it was the last straw. Always being told to wait. We'd had that for too long.' Certainly the mood of women changed in 1946. They *had* put up with shortages for too long. Their men were being demobilised and they wanted to look right for them. It has been suggested that had Churchill been able to swing factories into producing nylon yarn for stockings in 1945, he probably would not have lost the election to Attlee. That is how many of the dreams, hopes and beliefs which go to make up morale were tied up with their gauzy magic.

But there was no possibility of that. As the *Western Mail* said, 'Hopes that a limited number of British-made nylon stockings would be available in the shops early next spring are not likely to be realised. Factories engaged during the war in spinning nylon for parachutes...have not yet had time to switch... to the different type of yarn used in stocking manufacture.' It went on

Chanel photographed by Beaton in 1936. Ten years later, her popularity gone and her name in eclipse, she was in exile in Switzerland.

Far removed from the gilded halls of couture, people on Blackpool beach in 1947 concentrated on having the good time for which they had waited so long.

to condemn as 'wishful thinking' any hope that the situation might change within the year.

Nylons were *always* welcome, no matter from where. In an atmosphere of increasing protectionism as far as clothes were concerned, they were a rare exception. Not only the clothes but even the styles of other countries were condemned in what seems now to be nothing less than crude propagandist brain-washing. The *Glasgow Herald*'s fashion editor had this to say in 1945: '...say no to the American-sponsored low-neck short-skirted party dress. I have not seen one, but am quite certain that it does not make sense.' However, others took a more realistic view of the American influence. An advertisement for Sylvan Flakes washing powder ('You can tell them by their extra gentleness') read, 'I asked him to try to get me some undies. He got these in New York.' 'Oh! Who wouldn't be a sailor's girl!' is her friend's despairing cry. With the *Evening Standard* announcing that Mr Dalton had decided that, although clothes production would be increased 100 per cent in 1946, rationing would not only continue, but the points would remain at their previous level (forty-eight coupons per person per year in 1945), it was a cry likely to be echoed by many.

The first year of peace looked as if it would be as grim as the years of war. But at least things could be brightened up by a head scarf as the result of a bold initiative taken by the Czechoslovakian émigré fabric designers Zika and Lida Ascher, who had the idea of asking famous artists to design head scarves for them. Lida, the designer of the pair, had already worked with Molyneux, and she and her husband had realised the potential of fabrics designed specifically to attract the new young market for fashion-conscious clothes. Zika Ascher set up a company called Bourec, which took an aggressive approach to foreign sales. When the government-sponsored exhibition 'Britain Can Make It', aimed at spearheading the export drive, opened at the Victoria & Albert Museum, Ascher and Bourec were to the fore. Unlike virtually every other object on display, the fabrics were not labelled 'For Export Only' – a tag which soon had the added rider 'But Britain Can't Have It'.

From the success of these fabrics, some of which were chosen by Princess Elizabeth and Princess Margaret to be made up by Molyneux for dresses to be worn on the Royal Family's 1947

A snowy reunion for a North London family. Mrs Flo Martin in her best pinny and her daughters in Utility clothes pose with their demobbed son and brother.

Norman Hartnell preparing sketches for the royal tour of South Africa in 1947.

South African tour, Ascher moved in on Paris, where he was to set up an especially productive relationship with Christian Dior. At home, his artists' head scarves were almost instant collector's pieces, exhibited in art galleries, with a catalogue introduction by Sacheverell Sitwell, in which he claimed, 'A revolution has been accomplished in industrial design.' The list of artists who created the scarves was as impressive as it was eclectic: Henri Matisse and Henry Moore; Jean Cocteau and Christian Bérard; Anton Clavé and André Dérain; Ben Nicholson and Graham Sutherland; Marie Laurencin and Francis Picabia were some of the thirty-one who took part: the scarves were as successful artistically as they were commercially.

In the late Forties, London was battling to keep the fashion head start over Paris which the war had provided. Not everyone was sure the effort was worth it. Even Molyneux, the figurehead for London fashion during the hostilities, was convinced that Paris would regain its supremacy and he returned there to reopen his house in 1946.

It was not that British couturiers lacked talent. Indeed in the run-up years to the New Look it is possible to make a strong case for many of them having anticipated Christian Dior's 'bombshell'. Their crippling disadvantage was in the amount of material he had at his disposal in order to give his post-war fashion statement such emphasis that it was unavoidable – even if not as unique as is sometimes suggested.

It is not too far-fetched to suggest that the advantages gained by London as a fashion centre at couture level might have been maintained had the flow of fabric essential to the whole system been more freely available. In the Forties, as in pre-war days, a 'model' dress was just that – something to be used as a template or model for the copies to be made by the manufacturer or store buying the right to do so. At the top end of the model gown business, the client reproduced the original in precise detail, using the original material. So the dollar-earning potential of selling a couture dress to North America did not just benefit the couturier. It was a double earner when the fabric was taken into account – quite apart from keeping the looms busy.

The problem in post-war Britain was the time it took to implement the change from wartime to peacetime production; to re-establish skilled workers (many of whom

Special designs 'For Export Only', like these by Hartnell, kept London at the centre of the fashion world.

A dress made in fabric celebrating the first post-war Empire Games, held in 1946.

were still in the services) and train new 'hands'. Things were scarcely any better in Paris. *Vogue* reported in early 1945 that there was a chronic shortage of fabrics there and those available were mainly synthetic and so difficult to obtain that very few copies of dresses could be made. Silk stockings weren't just rare, they were shockingly expensive, costing at least £2 a pair. Quality of life had dropped even lower than in Britain. A chronic fuel shortage made laundering especially difficult: quite apart from the fact that the soap was ersatz, the water was cold and wet clothes lay around in unheated apartments for days before they dried. This was the time when a woman could not buy a lipstick unless she had an old case to hand in; and to buy a ring, she had to turn in an old one of exactly the same weight. Every effort was bent merely to keeping the country going and, in the clothing field, trying to supply the needs of the couture business – even by buying fabric from as far afield as China.

But the main advantage of Paris over London was the fact that government backing – which the British industry also had – was informed, whereas in Britain it was not. Non-austerity, 'for export only' fashion parades took place in London and attracted highly respectable orders in late 1945 and 1946. Buyers paid between 45 and 60 guineas (at least a third less than the prices in Paris) for the right to reproduce a model for their home markets, which stretched from Sweden and Switzerland to Canada and Australia. For this price they also received 'fabric reference' which told them the name of the fabric and gave details of the manufacturer who had made it. In this way, they could ensure that the model gown they would sell was an exact duplicate of the original. The system had been evolved in France and, before the war, had been responsible for building up that country's vast textile industry which would, very soon, become the power behind the New Look.

Alison Settle, writing in the *Observer* on 3 February 1946, exposed the weak link as being the lack of governmental grasp of the situation, allied to a fatal propensity to generate red tape:

'It is an extraordinary thing that even now officials, some at the Board of Trade itself, have no idea how this international trade functions. When one of the dress houses visited the Board to explain that there must be a licence granted for repeat fabric orders as each model was sold, an official readily agreed to release fabric...to the extent of 15 yards. He imagined that the transaction stopped with the sale of the model and was truly staggered to hear that what was required was not 15 yards but almost 15 *miles* of the Manchester cotton.

'Similarly, instead of the Board arranging for a covering licence for the purpose of this export effort, each designing firm has, *day by day* to apply (in triplicate) for every separate order received, whether for twenty models for an American store, two for Iraq or three from Scandinavia. The entire proceedings have to be restarted for each sale, not from any ill-will, but from lack of knowledge on the part of the officials concerned...officials have so long despised dress as a mere woman's frivolity that the idea of the couture being the shop window of the country's high class textile trade is to them completely strange. The Ministry of Labour, so soon as it recognised this as a national export movement, offered to have girl labour brought down from the North to help the creating houses, one of which was working with no more than five skilled hands. But when the firms explained that only labour with the high qualifications and experience in cutting, fitting, fine hand sewing and tailoring would be of use, no more was heard...'

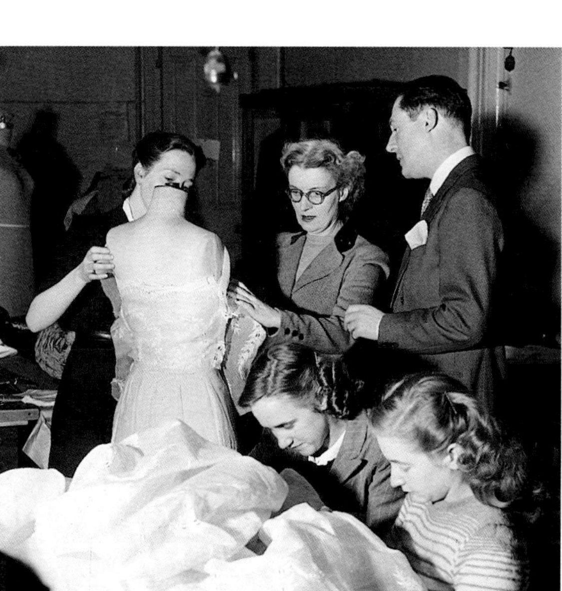

Hardy Amies, out of uniform, supervising a fitting at his newly founded fashion house in Savile Row.

Ten days later, in a radio programme for transmission around the world, Margaret Buchnell, describing the Hardy Amies show, commented, 'As I watched the foreign buyers going away they seemed to me to be purring.' The note of encouragement was taken up in the *Tatler* and *Bystander,* which wrote of the London couture collections, 'Remember these beautiful models represent the country's campaign for currency.' It needed to be said. Far too many officials and commentators contrasted the exquisite clothes shown to buyers with the drabness of their daily existence; measured the apparently hedonistic attitude to life which they exemplified against the coldest winter for years with inadequate heating, food, transport – in fact, inadequate *everything* – and puritanically refused to separate the artefact and

VE Day celebrations on 8 May 1945 – an opportunity to put on the best clothes you could muster and go out and have fun.

the purpose. To far too many, fashionable clothes were just a frivolous indulgence. This is hardly surprising, when even the Board of Trade could find no deeper purpose in them. It was the classic government 'Catch 22', wanting results without investment. The deficiencies were pointed out by *Vogue* when, writing of the London collections, it drew attention to the fact that 'the evening line is influenced by the magnificent silks and rayons from France...'

Away from the couture world, women were beginning to be demobilised, facing a return to 'civvy street' fraught with complications, including the question of dress. For many of them uniform had become almost second nature; they felt exposed and vulnerable when this carapace was removed and, for the first time in several years, they were expected to make their own choices about clothes. It was an intimate exercise which many of them had never had to perform, having left home – where mother made the dress decisions – at an early age to join an institution where there were no decisions to be made at the individual level. The authorities were sensitive to the problem and efforts were made to ease the transition to ordinary life.

Women's magazines were full of helpful articles for the 4½ million women still in uniform at the end of the war, the majority of whom were about to leave the services. Hints on prices: 'Filmy underclothes of which you have dreamed,' *Vogue* told them, 'now cost as much as a pre-war evening dress.' There were other shocks. Tailors were so short-handed that even basic alterations were liable to take from six to nine months. Invisible menders were at a premium, especially for repairs to the all-precious nylons. It was a feature of many dry cleaners to see girls sitting in the window to get maximum light for this precise and tiring work. The average charge per run, normally regardless of length, was 1s 3d which, although a far from negligible sum to most women, was considered money well spent compared to the cost – not to mention the difficulty – of buying a new pair. Finding nylons was not only a constant preoccupation; for some women it almost reached the level of obsession: 'You'd hear a rumour from a friend who worked in a shop whenever a consignment was due,' a woman in the West Midlands said. 'I remember once, I got up early and got round to the shop by about quarter to seven in the morning. The queue was six deep and went right round the building. I waited but was too far back. They'd all gone long before I got anywhere near the door.' There were reports of queues 1,000 strong in Leeds and Bradford whenever a consignment arrived. It was almost as if nylons had a miraculous power to make women sexually attractive. Certainly, by the late Forties, few women felt they could compete in glamour or sex if they *didn't* wear nylons. For demobbed women, buying a pair was an essential rite of passage into the civilian world.

The major shops in most cities began to create window displays especially designed to ease women back into civilian life and, of course, persuade them to use the coupons on their special demobilisation cards with them. In the West End John Lewis employed advisers to show demobbed women the new lines in clothes and furniture, and Selfridges held a services' dress parade every Friday at 3pm during September and October 1945. It began with a beauty talk, lasting about five minutes, followed by a parade of Utility fashions showing two sample wardrobes, each totalling between £8 and £10, consisting of either a coat, dress and overall or a suit, blouse and mackintosh. Some shops with women billeted nearby staged special mannequin parades at their units, again showing what could be bought in the way of a wardrobe within certain coupon – and price – restrictions. To overcome both, many firms were prepared to dye and alter uniforms so that they could be used as civilian suits.

It wasn't easy for either side. Women found it hard to readjust to a civilian life so different from the one they had romanticised in their memory. The difficulties over clothing were recognised as being a major cause of depression. To many, the shortages seemed even more severe than during the war. 'If it wasn't unobtainable,' one woman told me, 'there was always a waiting list. It shouldn't have mattered, really, but it did. We had won the war and still everything went on just like before.'

She wasn't correct. Things were loosening up daily but an almost total clamp-down on production of civilian clothing could not be lifted quickly. Not only were many of the workers required for full-scale production still in the services, the vital raw materials were not available in the quantity required for anything even approaching the mass-production levels of pre-war output. But attitudes were changing: after the wartime urgency, when any dress was acceptable as long as the individual appeared for work, offices and shops began to reimpose pre-war dress codes, often with unexpected side effects. A newspaper report told of a woman who worked in the perfume department of a West End store. She was tactfully told that her dress would not do now that the war was over.

Demobilisation, the fateful day when uniform was exchanged for 'civvies' and the dress problems of civilian life had to be faced.

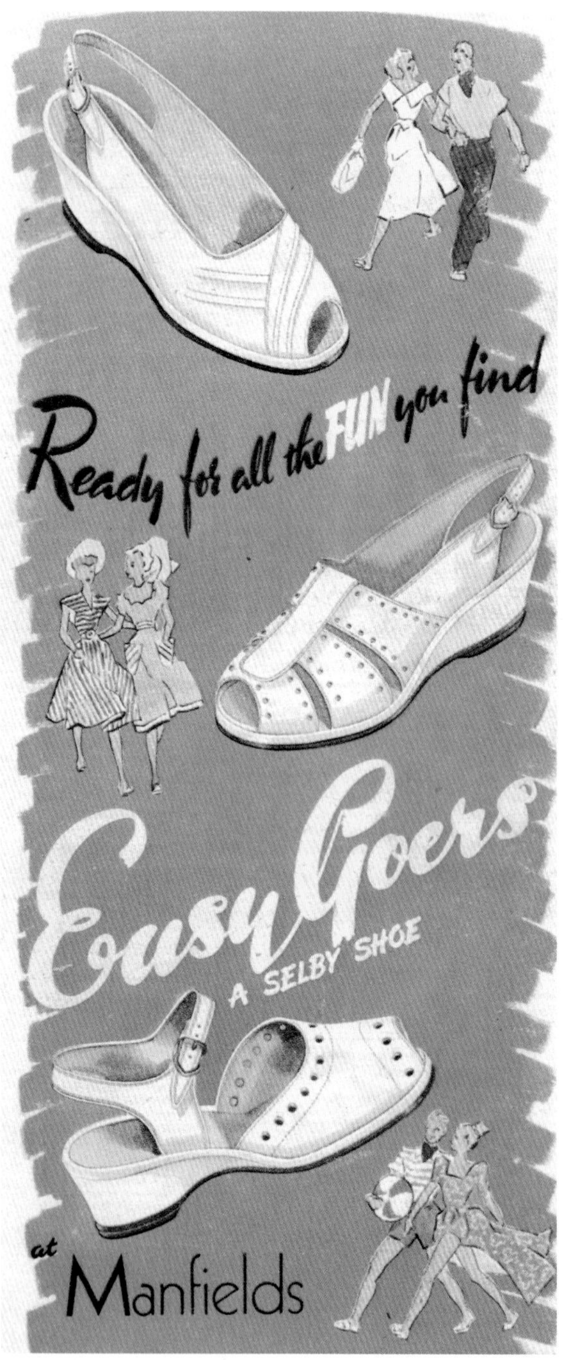

Ready for all the FUN you find
Easy Goers
A SELBY SHOE
at Manfields

Light-coloured sling-back sandals with peep toes were a great post-war fad.

It was shabby and her shoes were badly in need of repair. In desperation to keep the job, she bought some black market coupons, paying the considerable sum of £2 for them. When she presented them, they were detected as forgeries. Desperate, she asked the newspaper what she could do: 'If I'm not smartly dressed, I'll lose my job, and I simply cannot manage on four coupons a month.' It was a cry with which thousands of women could identify.

Morale was not helped by the letters which began arriving from GI brides. Although many of them found it extremely difficult to adapt to the American way of life, all of them were amazed at how freely available fashionable clothes were. American ready-to-wear was altogether sassier, snappier and sexier than its European and British counterparts. Above all, it was younger. In fact, it is a truism that the move to lower the fashionable age to well below thirty began in America in the late Forties. It was more than a mere sea change: it was a psychological realignment and it stemmed from the huge rise in numbers of girls going to college, which coincided with the beginning of the boom in middle-class wealth which was to give Americans the highest standard of living in the world by the mid-Fifties.

Young fashion, American style, was fun fashion, born from the nation's love of sport and bred by a determination to be as casual and unstuffy as was consistent with the demands of law, order and decency. From the turned-under bob and page-boy hairstyles, requiring little more than a quick comb-through for the day, to the well-fitting penny loafers and saddle shoes, American college looks were about health and fitness. Unlike their counterparts across the Atlantic, American girls had the help of an abundance of home-grown fruit and vegetables; meat and milk in full supply and, already, the first stirrings of a vitamin pill industry which was to grow into a billion-dollar concern. But there was something else about young

American women which made their appearance so attractive: they weren't just healthy, they were happy. They were in charge of their lives, felt equal to men and, above all, had the vigour which years of rationing and restriction had weakened in Britain's young women.

Gor-Ray skirts were so smart and long-lasting that there were waiting lists for them immediately after the war.

We are talking of a phenomenon which hardly existed outside America and certainly had not yet been named beyond its shores. It was in the Forties that the teenager appeared and the cult of the adolescent began – encouraged by the commercial potential manufacturers could foresee in defining and divorcing this sub-genre from the main commercial species. In no time at all teenagers had their own music, their own demotic and, inevitably, their own fashion industry. Between 1944 and 1946, Minx Modes, a 'junior' fashion manufacturer sold over $12m worth of frocks. By 1949 even a staid and very 'grown up' magazine like *Ladies' Home Journal* had a section called 'Profile of Youth'. Teenage girls dressed as 'sports', in rolled-up jeans, 'Sloppy Joe' sweaters, over-sized shirts worn hanging out, duffle coats, alpaca teddy-bear coats and ankle socks. Tartan skirts under parkas were a craze for college girls when they weren't wearing Argyll-knit sweaters and baseball jackets. In essence they were revelling in dressing like surrogate boys but, when dating began, they changed to prim and pristine American cotton, crisp and clean.

Their sisters in their mid or late twenties were doing much the same thing on a more sophisticated level, following the lead of a young designer who, like Adrian earlier, was having a huge influence and was to have more effect on the fashion attitudes of the next forty years than anyone in Paris in the Forties, with the exception

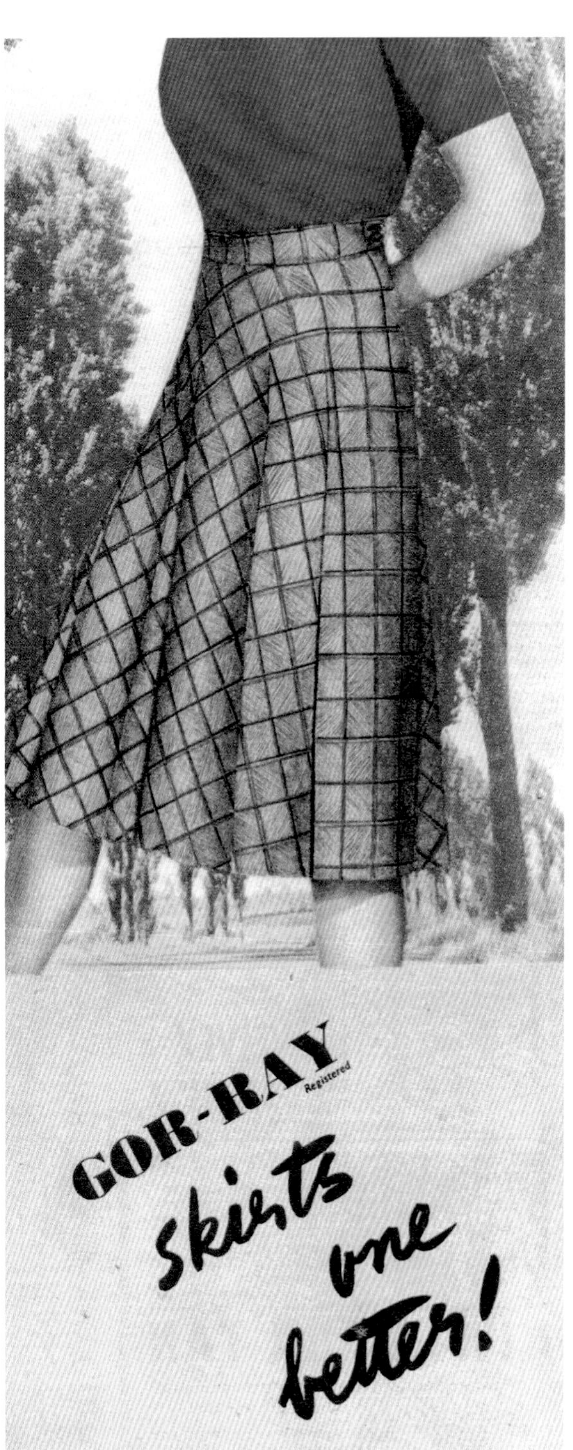
GOR-RAY
Registered
skirts one better!

ABOVE AND LEFT: With these designs from the 1940s, Claire McCardell envisaged modern sportswear and its importance twenty-five years ahead of the rest.

Although this Claire McCardell dress was designed in 1946, it could be worn today and seem perfectly fashionable.

of Balenciaga. Claire McCardell began working for the Seventh Avenue manufacturer Townley Frocks, Inc., in 1941. By the end of the war, she had evolved her philosophy of dress. Unadorned, non-status, sporting and based on 'unsophisticated' fabrics such as cotton jersey and chambray, her clothes eschewed padding, built-in bras, light corsets and all decorative detailing apart from top-stitching, for a natural line which followed that of the body. It sounds naive, even simplistic, but was in fact highly sophisticated in what McCardell left unstated. These were clothes for modern, independent women. Fundamental and functional as Philip Johnson's New Canaan glass house, they were not only timeless but still ahead of the rest years later. An exhibition of McCardell's work in Los Angeles in 1953 showed clothes designed over a period of twenty years. Every one was as wearable then – and would be as wearable today – as when first designed, years earlier. As McCardell said, 'Fashions earn their right to survive by continuing to play the same role.'

One of the people who best understood Dior's approach was fashion artist René Gruau, whose elegant line was to animate fashion magazines for the next forty-odd years.

Although this was the future, Britain and Europe were barely aware of it. Their designers were busy creating clothes for a different sort of status. Whereas McCardell's clothes elevated fitness, health and independence of spirit, theirs were concerned with wealth and class, a fact acknowledged by *Life* magazine with its comment, 'Nobody looks as born to a ball gown as does the British lady.' High fashion and its promulgators are essentially old-fashioned. They try to keep the status quo – in class as well as clothes – unruffled as long as possible. That is the reason why Britain and France eventually lost the fashion lead to America. Their designers were unaware that a new breed of woman was brewing, a breed which was not prepared to be trussed up and gilded in order to correspond to outdated class and sexual mores. And they were helped in their ostrich approach by the phenomenal success of the New Look, which took fashion back, rather than moving it forward.

Fashion historians tend to skip over the Forties as a period of stasis suddenly reanimated by the New Look, before moving on quickly to the Fifties. In fact the Forties were a pivotal point for fashion and femininity. They were the background to a conflict the outcome of which led to a completely

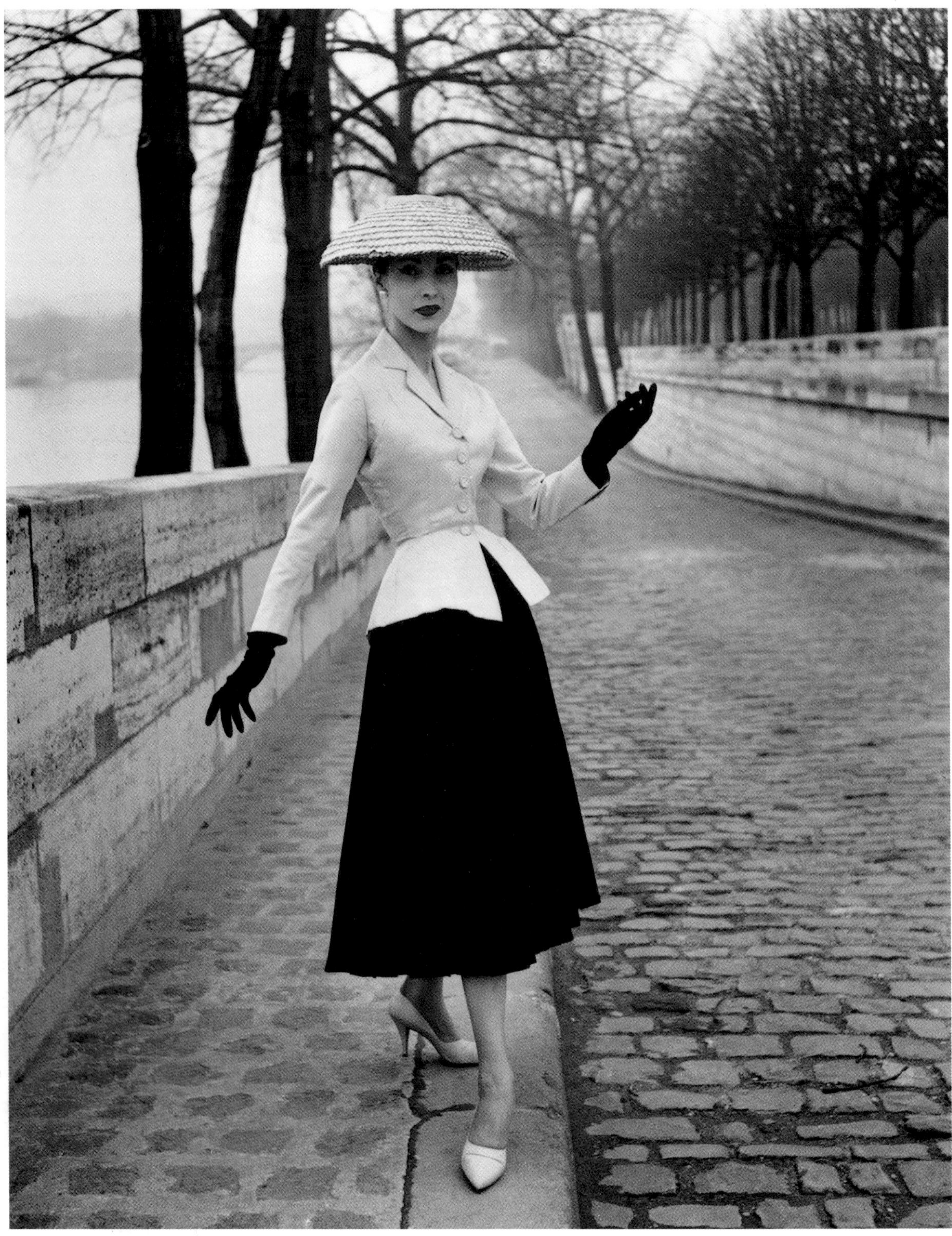

new approach to and by women, culminating in the Women's Lib Movement and the changed relationship between the sexes which is *the* characteristic of the last years of the twentieth century.

The fight was over sex appeal, and what form it should take. At its extremities were Claire McCardell and, facing her over a credibility and comprehension gap as wide as the Atlantic, Christian Dior. Practicality and ease versus romanticism and glamour; the old world versus the new; the male designer versus the female: there are many catchphrases which can pinpoint the conflict. And it was a conflict – of fundamental ideology as well as social balance.

Initially, designers in Europe and Britain followed Dior, not necessarily because they were as overwhelmed by the New Look as journalists and public were, but because they could see in it the logical continuation of their own thoughts in the late Thirties and even during the war. It is a truism that, far from being a new look, what Dior created was the current look given enormous impact by the scale and proportions of his clothes. The facts are beyond dispute: 'Hips are important and discreetly padded....waists are small with clever cutting and seaming to make them smaller...a softly rounded shoulderline...skirts eighteen inches from the ground...the impression of a pyramid, with width at the skirt hem and the line tapering towards the shoulders...' A journalist's description of the clothes presented by Dior on 12 February 1947, commonly known as The New Look? No, Hardy Amies' press notes for his own collection, presented in January 1946.

The start of it all. 'Bar', the first New Look suit of 1947, with a jacket in palest pink shantung and a skirt in black wool crepe.

The new mood also became apparent in Paris. The October 1946 edition of *Vogue* commented, 'In this autumn's Paris collections clothes were fabulous...a subtle yielding to feminine lines, the lines of 1910 and thereabouts...tight little waists... rounded, almost Rubens-rounded hips... In Paris this autumn every designer seemed intoxicated with the feminine atmosphere...' Even in March 1947, barely a month after Dior's show, *Vogue* could still write, 'Paris develops current trends; makes no revolutionary

A New Look cocktail dress by Dior. The skirt required a shockingly extravagant 15 yards of material.

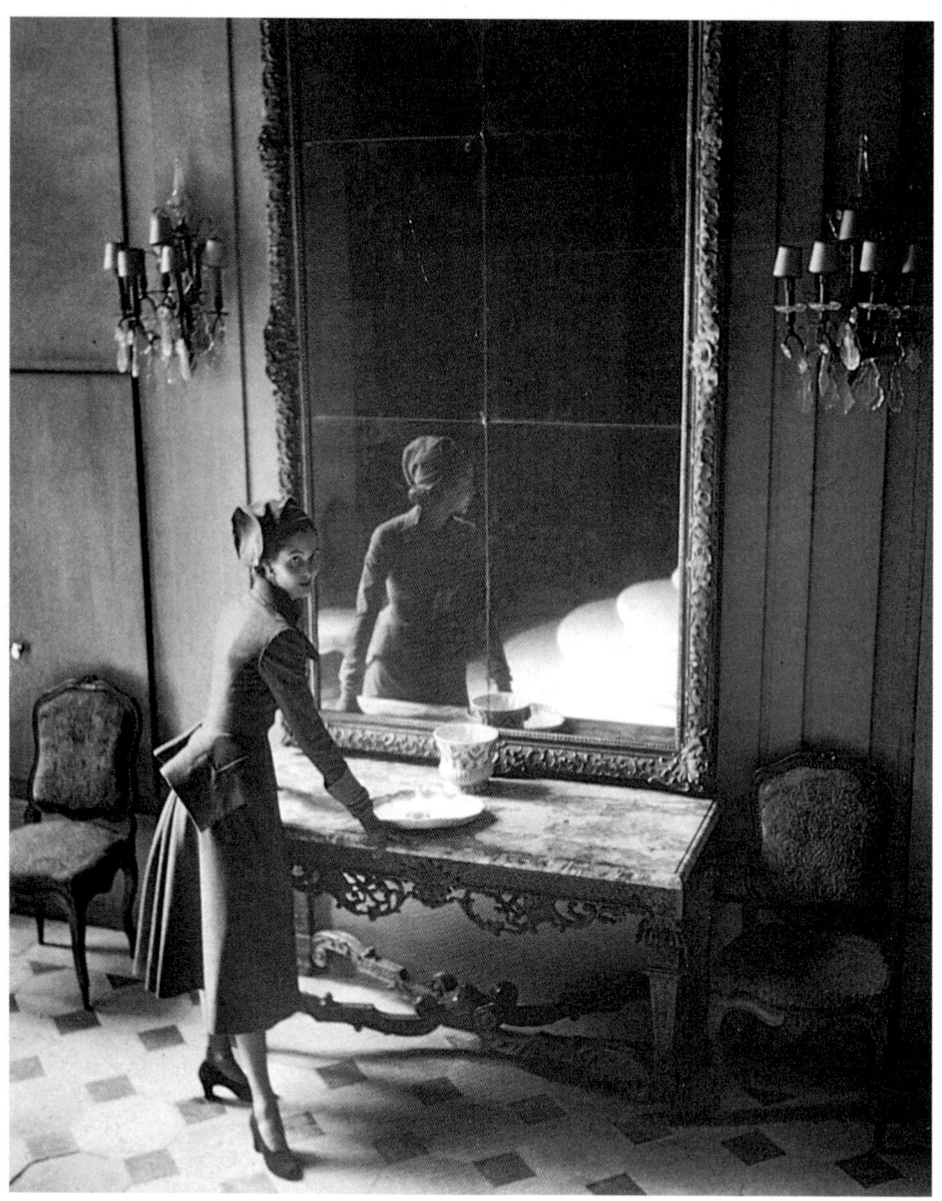

ABOVE: An elegant suit from Dior's 'Zig-Zag' collection. RIGHT: A Dior ball-gown, at its best in a grand setting.

The New Look was a gift to artists. Eric captures the Dior spirit in a few assured lines.

breakaways, shows nothing that puts our present clothes right out of court.. P.S. The season's sensation is the new house of Christian Dior...' The following month the magazine wrote of him, 'Dior uses fabric lavishly in skirts – fifteen yards in a woollen day dress, twenty-five yards in a short taffeta evening dress. He pads these pleated skirts with stiff cambric; builds corsets and busts into the dresses so that they practically stand alone...'

In September, reporting on the London Collections, the *Vogue* headline was 'Day skirts drop dramatically' and the October issue, reporting Paris, showed how quickly the New Look had been taken to extremes, with skirt lengths anything from 14 to 8 inches from the floor and, below the waist 'a supernaturally rounded line – what is currently called the "derrière de Paris".' The New Look had arrived – a fact not universally pleasing.

Alison Settle considered that many men were wondering 'if the designers have lost both sense and sensibility as well as their self-critical faculty?...What sort of clothes are these for today's active and restless life?...Women able to pay for them show no conscience in a world suffering from a grave textile famine...it is not to be expected, at this particular juncture in our history, that the women of Britain will be able to alter their wardrobe at the dictation of fashion. They will be fortunate if coupons run to one coat or suit.' She ended by condemning 'the lines of today' as 'long, heavy and even middle-aged'.

Miss Settle was not alone in her criticism. Mabel Ridleigh, MP for North Ilford, Essex, chose her words carefully for her comments. Knowing, so soon after the war, the emotive power of the word 'dictator', she wrote in the *Daily Herald*, 'I hope that fashion dictators will realise the new outlook of women and give the death blow to any attempt at curtailing their freedom.' Dame Anne Loughlin regretted that 'time, labour, materials and money should be wasted on these imbecilities'. Marjorie Beckett, writing in *Picture Post* under the heading 'Paris Forgets This Is 1947', saw the effects of the New Look as likely to move women back to 'the indolent and wealthy years before the 1914 war... when fashion was the prerogative of the leisured wealthy woman, and not the everyday concern of typist, saleswoman or housewife.'

It seems remarkable today how thinly class resentment was disguised in much of the New Look criticism, but the comments must be measured against the wave of egalitarianism which swept Britain after the war. There was enormous idealism; a real belief that civilisation must be based not merely on putative but on practical democracy. Privilege and irresponsibility fitted awkwardly with the new world being brought into being by Mr Attlee's Labour Government – a world of free education and a state-funded system of welfare aimed at bringing at least a measure of social balance for the good of the majority.

It wasn't just that the clothes in the form in which they were shown in Paris seemed so impractical that only the privileged, who neither went to work nor relied on public transport, could wear them. There was a deeper distrust. The clothes required so much material – over 40 metres in some cases – that only the rich could afford them. In a country like Britain, ideologically puritan, it seemed against all the new tenets that wealth should be available for such extravagance, merely to gratify vanity. People in post-war Britain were still morally outraged by the profits made by spivs, profiteers and 'dodgers'. It seemed to many that the new fashion could be paid for only by such 'dirty' money. Even when that wasn't the case, such flaunting, outrageously extravagant clothes were seen by many as the outward and visible sign that, given half a chance, the rich upper classes would revert to their old ways like a shot. In one of her letters, Nancy Mitford – more aware of class attitudes than many – wrote from Paris 'Have you heard about the New Look? You pad your hips and squeeze your waist and skirts are to the ankle it is bliss....and people shout ordures at you from vans because for some reason it creates class feeling in a way no sables could.' She was right and it was because, in the aftermath of war, the New Look was too luxurious, too unattainable by the majority to do anything else. It was seen as a political gesture of defiance from the rich to the poor. To the millions of refugees and dispossessed, it suggested the indifference to the rest which the aristocracy had so often shown in the past.

When naive people talk of the New Look saving fashion they fail to realise that fashion has no meaning unless it is linked with the realities of daily life. What the New Look did was to divorce couture from the rest of the world – a situation which is still so today. The immediate effect of the New Look – at a crucial moment when ready-to-wear was just burgeoning – was to shunt it off on to the plateau of unreality where it became something to gawp at, be amused by, even moved by, but essentially irrelevant. The ultimate legacy of Dior's bombshell was to make Paris fashion so frivolous in many eyes that women turned to London in the Sixties, Milan in the Seventies and New

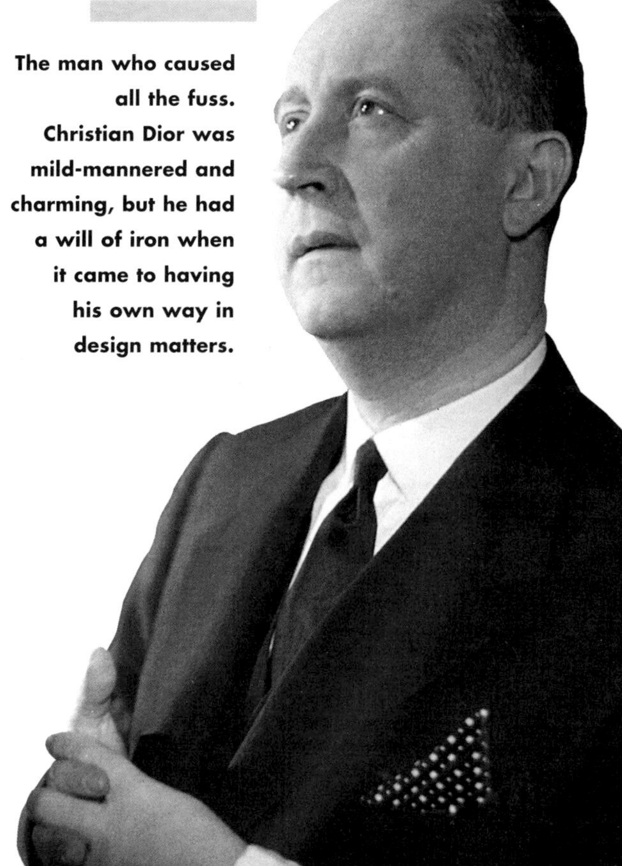

The man who caused all the fuss. Christian Dior was mild-mannered and charming, but he had a will of iron when it came to having his own way in design matters.

York in the Eighties, leaving the city of couture to perform the role of bread and circuses for the media. After Dior, Paris fashion exchanged being a real fashion influence for the extravagance and drama which sells perfumes and cosmetics rather than clothes. Dior castrated Paris fashion and initiated its long descent into sterility because he forgot the realities of life for real women – as was to be expected of the man whose views were so blinkered that he could write in his biography, *Dior by Dior*, 'When I opened my house, I told M. Boussac [his backer] that I wanted to dress only the most fashionable women, from the first ranks of society.'

The New Look became highly exaggerated in Dior's second collection of 1947. Almost as if, having tested the waters, he had satisfied himself that he could get away with more than he originally dared, it was in his subsequent collections that he dropped the hemline almost to ankle length and filled out the skirts with horsehair and canvas to create a look of such extravagance that it had actually become the *new* look, with a diminishing connection with previous Forties fashion and an increasing compulsion for everyone else to follow.

And they did, at every level. Despite the fact that the look was becoming more theatrical and unreal with each collection, ready-to-wear manufacturers could ignore it no longer. Regardless of government edicts, shortage of material and the exigencies of rationing, New Look copies began to appear in shops and stores. The British firm Dereta produced a non-Utility New Look suit in grey flannel in an edition of 700 and sold out entirely within two weeks. By comparison with today's sales figures this seems unremarkable, but it was an amazing statistic at the time. Such a dramatic fashion change represented commercial disaster for many manufacturers, who could see their present stock becoming so out-of-date that it would soon be unsaleable.

For those who could swing quickly into production, the New Look was the imaginative leap for which the fashion industry had been waiting. By the middle of 1948, it had developed to such an extent that clothes designed as recently as early 1947 looked hopelessly *démodé*. It was like a blow from a sledgehammer, beating out a repetitious and unavoidable slogan: 'Throw away the old; on with the new.' The only women who could fully follow its edict were the Americans, free of the restrictions in Europe and with considerably more disposable income. With US *Vogue* and *Harper's Bazaar* featuring nothing but the New Look, thousands of them swung over to it, although there were little pockets of resistance. In Dallas, 1,300 women felt strongly enough to join a 'Little Below the Knee Club', but it was a gimmick which survived barely long enough to get into the newspapers. A Louisville office girls' petition managed to gather only 676 signatures. The impact of the New Look swept all opposition aside.

Claire McCardell shows the modern way to dress romantically, without the corsets, padded hips or horsehair underskirts of the New Look.

It took less than three months for Seventh Avenue to begin producing American New Look lines. They were the triumph of an industry as modern in production techniques as it was alert to nuances in the mood of American women. Whilst Europe – still in hapless disarray from the war – was slowly cranking up again in production, American manufacturers, streamlined and efficient, were racing ahead. Their speedy reaction to the need for the New Look was impressive: not only were New Look copies in the stores nationwide, they were at highly competitive prices. A copy of a Dior creation costing $500 in France was often sold on Main Street, USA, for less than $20.

Without the enthusiasm of the American press and mass-market manufacturers, it is unlikely that

Dior's fashion statement would have rampaged so triumphantly around the world. That it did so put Paris firmly in the lead again. The very industry which should have been encouraging its own couturiers and designers – the Claire McCardells – was guilty of putting their contribution to fashion on hold for several years. It wasn't just the shock of the new, it was also the thrill of the exotic. American women had felt small-town and cut off during the war whilst, at the same time, becoming aware of the world – through the movements of GI brothers and husbands – as never before. They wanted the sophistication of French fashion and perfume, just as the Upper Crust had in the years before the war. But this was now a massive ground swell and it had to be accommodated. The forecast of the *Boston Christian Science Monitor* in 1946 that 'well-dressed American women will buy their costumes impartially either side of the Atlantic' was contradicted by the facts of 1947 and the years immediately following. One woman, now dead, who worked in the US rag trade for many years, told me that, in her opinion, this love of everything French created snobbery where magazine editors and the fashion trade imagined they were creating style: 'Women from des Moines, or wherever, *had* to vacation in Europe during the Fifties and their first stop was Paris, France. Before they'd unpacked, they were round 30 avenue Montaigne being fitted for that once-in-a-lifetime ball gown – for des Moines! – with the Dior label.'

The hysteria had begun almost immediately. In September 1947 Dior was awarded an 'Oscar' by the Dallas department store Nieman Marcus, along with Norman Hartnell and Ferragamo, the Italian shoemaker. He travelled to Texas to accept it personally and, incidentally, receive massive media coverage. Everyone in the US had heard of Dior; now, thanks to television, they all knew what he looked like, how he moved, the tone of his voice – all the personalising things so good for sales. He became that thing beloved of all Americans – the guy famous for being famous. No wonder sales boomed.

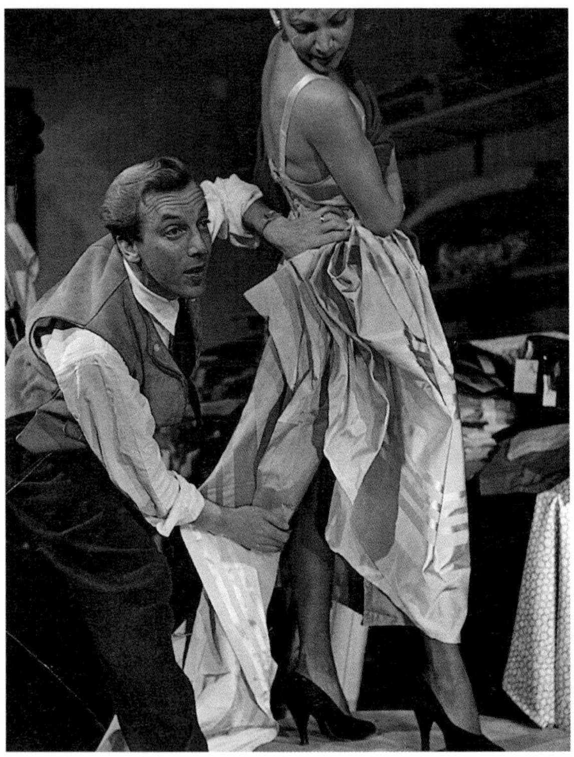

Jacques Fath, apart from Dior the only designer in Paris with sound backing, was a major figure who died tragically young.

Dior really couldn't fail. Quite apart from the enthusiasm of the Americans he was lucky in his backer. Marcel Boussac provided virtually unlimited capital as well as a highly experienced administrative staff to help Dior. His initial investment of 10 million francs had been multiplied by ten by 1949. Boussac was a man of vision, as well as a shrewd operator in the textile business. A racehorse owner and breeder, he sold many of his stable to Americans so that he could deposit considerable amounts in dollar accounts there – which were useful when, in 1948, to avoid restrictive taxes levied on foreign-manufactured goods by the American Government, he was able to set up Christian Dior-New York to manufacture its own ready-to-wear lines in America.

No one had such a head start as Dior. His fellow French designer Jacques Fath, who signed a contract with an American manufacturer, Joseph Halpert, giving the firm the exclusive right to produce his designs in America for ready-to-wear, was a rarity in Paris in the late Forties in that he had neither backer nor debts and his business was booming. Everybody else had to fight to keep up. London couture especially felt the pinch. Of the original Fashion Group of Great Britain, founded with such high hopes before the war, few now remained. The Group had been rechristened in 1942 and it was as the Incorporated Society of London Fashion Designers that it was agreed that London collections would be shown to transatlantic and other buyers in the week before the French shows in the hope of catching them before their cheque-books were ravaged in the magic of Paris. With Molyneux back in Paris and Hartnell renowned more for his royal connections than his originality, the Group would have looked pale indeed had not Hardy Amies taken such a positive approach to American sales. His first post-war trip to the United States, in 1946, brought in $8,000's worth of orders and this commitment remained with him for the next four years.

Of the rest, there was no one who could be called a major talent, capable of holding his own on an international stage. Some, like Peter Russell, Victor Stiebel and Digby Morton, were good, if derivative, designers. Of others, such as Bianca Mosca, Elspeth Champcommunal and Angele Delanghue, it can only be said that they produced attractive clothes which appealed to their private clients, as the clothes of good dressmakers always have. None could attract the American interest. One of the effects of the New Look which put London at a disadvantage was the fact that Dior's clothes were so soft and feminine. For day wear, dresses became the focus of attention, taking away interest in the staple of London couture, the immaculately tailored tweed suit. For evening, London was so entirely upstaged by the magnificence and glamour of Paris that it could only follow at a respectful distance, echoing the shape and form but entirely lacking the magnificence of beading and embroidery at which Paris was unbeatable. It was no wonder, as the American market deserted them and the skills of Paris reached

Anna Neagle in *Maytime in Mayfair,* a hymn of praise to London high fashion in 1949.

Evening dresses by the New York-based couturier Charles James show that Dior was not the only one in love with the heady romance of richly draped and precious fabrics.

'Cross-currents', a 1949 silk dress by Hardy Amies, showing the influence of the New Look on London fashion.

magnificent heights in the early Fifties, that most of the London couturiers were gradually forced to close down.

Although in no sense a powerhouse of haute couture, London undoubtedly suffered from the snobbery attached to a Paris label. It had always existed but, after the New Look, 'a Paris gown' was *de rigueur* for any woman wishing to be entirely in the fashion. British fashion magazines of the late Forties and early Fifties are full of photographs of elegant, wearable clothes by designers such as Mattli, Michael Sherard, Ronald Paterson and John Cavenagh – who had worked with Molyneux and created the wedding dresses of the Duchess of Kent and Princess Alexandra. But their work evinced diminishing interest abroad even though its dollar-earning capacity – small as it was – was appreciated by Harold Wilson, President of the Board of Trade. In an introduction to a joint show of the London fashion designers, he mentioned

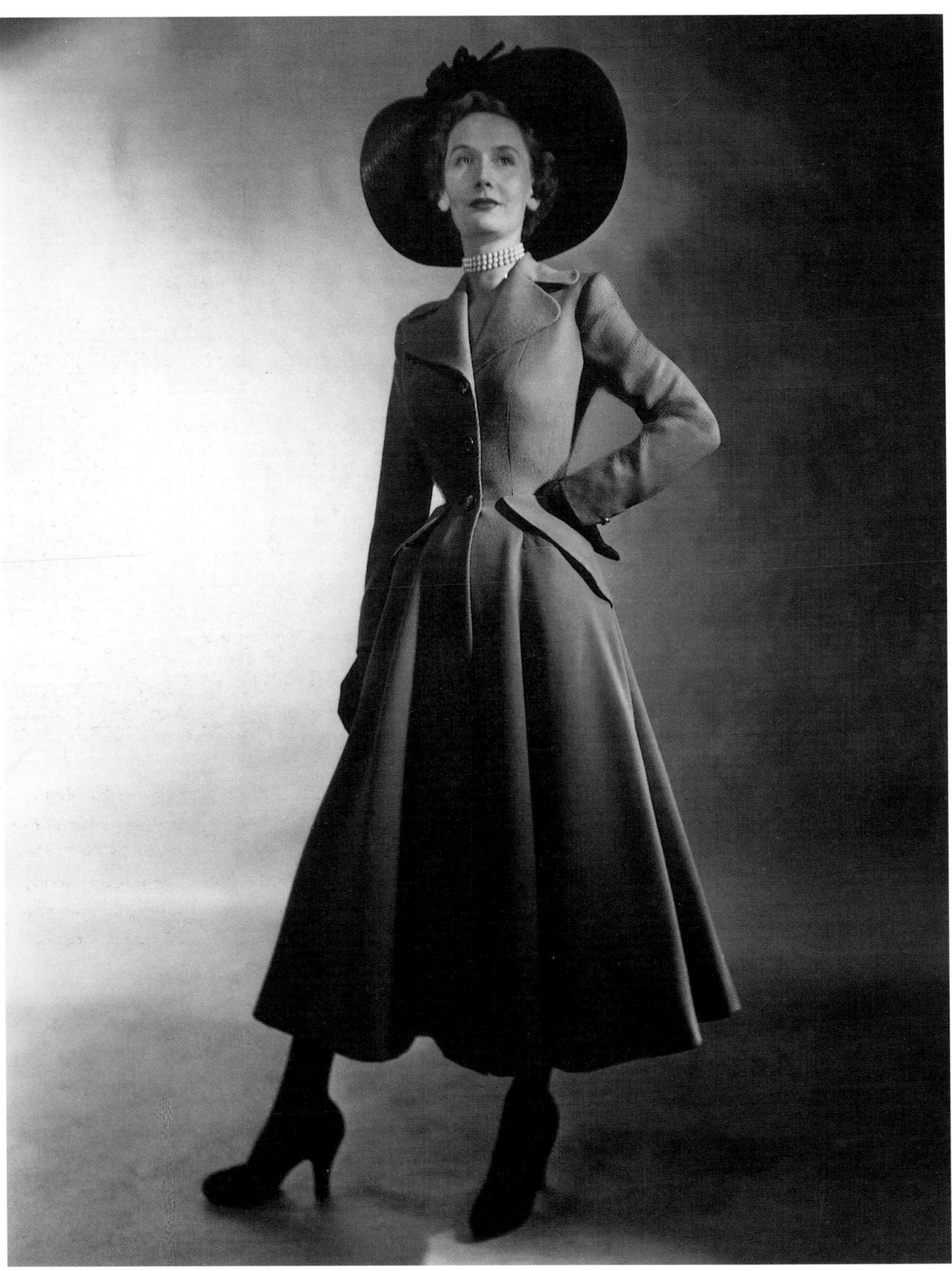

As this consummately cut coat shows, Hardy Amies was the London couturier who most fully understood Dior's approach. Both were craftsmen who saw the nobility of their trade as, in Amies's words, 'doing honour to cloth'.

their 'distinctive contribution to world fashion'. But fashion insiders were less positive. The days when beautiful clothes for elegant lives were an end in themselves had gone. The hugely expanding American ready-to-wear system demanded more than that. Ideas were what it required. Brilliantly innovative ideas of the kind found only in Paris.

In *The Happy Years*, a selection of his diaries from the Forties, Cecil Beaton encapsulated the difference. 'After trying to instil some sort of allure into my photographs of the "stick in the mud" dowdiness of "London couturiers",' he wrote after a photographic session featuring Paris designs, 'these clothes give me wings. Balenciaga's line... so rich and luxurious that it is stimulating just to see it.' Nobody but the most partisan would have dreamed of writing so lyrically of London fashion. The New Look had effectively destroyed any hopes that British couture ever had of becoming a world player. But, just as it stimulated the American ready-to-wear business, so it had its effect on British manufacturers. By 1949, a modified but very recognisable version was in most shops and women could even make it themselves. *Weldon's Ladies Journal* that year offered a cut out and ready to sew New Look dress for 35s and seven coupons.

Even so, there were pockets of resistance motivated as much by social and political attitudes as by fashion approaches. A Midlands woman told me, 'It was always a rich woman's fashion. Ordinary women didn't have the life – the occasions – for it. Mind you, it *was* beautiful.' Another

Princess Elizabeth with the King at the Derby in 1948. Her appearance clearly shows the influence of the New Look.

did wear it. 'It was lovely,' she recalls. 'So romantic. I had a lovely almond green coat with a small rounded collar, six double buttons, then this enormous skirt. I felt like a Queen! What was funny was how you stood. It was different. I felt different in it. Straighter. Taller. Even my best friend couldn't call me elegant, but that coat – it was by Slimma – was the nearest I ever got to it!' Even in its cheapest versions, this was head-turning fashion which, in the first few months, electrified the High Street: 'I remember we were in Swansea one Saturday morning and suddenly there was this girl walking towards us in a red coat.

For the Royal Wedding in 1947 Hartnell designed Princess Elizabeth's wedding dress and the outfits of most of the family and principal guests.

Everybody was looking, stopped, staring really. My friend and I both said that it was too extreme for ordinary wear, but by the same time next year we were wearing it and *loving* it. Everybody was, who was young, in Swansea.' And Birmingham, Manchester, Newcastle, Glasgow – wherever there were women who wanted to be in the fashion.

Even Princess Elizabeth wore it on an official visit to France and was commended for her elegance by Dior himself. She and her sister, Princess Margaret, were fashion leaders in the Forties. Everyone from débutantes to factory girls eagerly followed how they dressed and tried to obtain the same effect. The interest in everything they did reached its high point with Princess Elizabeth's marriage in November 1947. Her wedding dress was designed along traditional lines by Norman Hartnell. Much as it was admired, it had little relevance to fashion for the majority. Women were much more interested in – in some cases, obsessed with – her trousseau, especially her 'going away' outfit. Would it be New Look?

It was not. Instead, Hartnell designed a modest and distinctly matronly coupon-controlled dress in 'love-in-the-mist' blue crepe. It had a cross-over bodice, draped to the left hip, a straight skirt with trim side panels and a hemline 14 inches from the ground. It had a matching velour coat and a high beret-type bonnet trimmed with ostrich feathers, designed by Aage Thaarup, the royal milliner.

Copies of the dress were on sale in Oxford Street within ten days.

Following so soon after the New Look, the Royal Wedding was another example of how women's role was seen in the post-war years. Femininity was required by men, and by many women, after the Rosie the Riveter years of hard, dirty industrial work. It was reaction to all of that which gave the New Look its impact. Schiaparelli, exceptionally scathing as she felt that it had swept away the military look which she claimed as her own, remarked that, 'cleverly planned and magnificently financed', the New Look benefited from 'the greatest din of publicity ever known' and had 'the shortest life of any fashion in history'. In fact, it had a longer run than most fashion, for the very reasons for which she castigated it. The paradox is that, after the initial impact on Paris, the publicity 'din' was largely created not in France but in America, where post-war comsumerism required just such an uncompromising, all-embracing manner in order to get fashion buying cranked up again.

Yet it was America which was in the forefront of fashion thinking with its casual, sporting approach to dress, and France which would have to come in line with US design attitudes which created the bedrock of fashion in the past fifty years: the concept of separates without which jogging clothes, sweats, siren suits, tank tops and all the other sports-related items which *are* fashion to the majority could not have come about. And, just as American enthusiasm for the New Look had made it a fashion, so, when Chanel returned, determined to stop the reign of Dior, of whose work she said, 'It looks good, but it isn't real,' it was the US fashion journalists who understood the unconstrained, relaxed elegance of her suits which, unlike anything created by Dior at the time, can still be worn today as fashion, with no hint of period dress.

For all the beautiful clothes of the New Look – and there were many – it is hard to argue with the assessment of Madge Garland, fashion editor of *Vogue*, when she wrote that it was 'the afterglow of the sunset of French taste'. But perhaps it is kinder to allow the man who pleased so many women to have the final word: 'To make a woman feel better, you must make her feel beautiful.' Patronising as such a remark is, it found its answering chord.

A *Vogue* cover from late 1946, before the New Look 'bombshell', shows that Dior's approach was not as unique as it was made out to be.

INDEX

Page numbers in *italic* refer to picture captions

Picture Acknowledgements

Grateful thanks are due to the Departments of Art, Exhibitions, Marketing and Trading, Photographs and Printed Books at the Imperial War Museum and to the lenders or donors of items photographed, and to Andrea Heselton and Angelo Hornak for special photography.

British Film Institute courtesy MGM 96

British Film Institute courtesy UGC (UK) 183

Camera Press/Cecil Beaton 25, 26, 159

Condé Nast Publications Ltd/ American Vogue 175 (photo Blumenfeld)
Condé Nast Publications Ltd/British Vogue 13 (photo Horst), 18 (photo Eliascheff), 19 (Francis Marshall), 20 (photo Glass), 21 (photo A. O'Neill), 29 (photo Steichen), 30 (photo Horst), 31 (René Bouchée), 37 (photo Horst), 38 (René Bouet-Willaumez), 81 (Francis Marshall), 91TL (photo Cecil Beaton), 100, 102R, 110 (photo Cecil Beaton), 122 (J. Pages), 126 (photo Horst), 151 (photo Cecil Beaton), 176 (photo Coffin), 177 (photo Coffin), 178 (Eric), 189 (photo Horst)

The Fashion Research Centre, Bath 93, 173

Collection du Conservatoire des Créations Hermès, Paris 158

Hulton Getty 8, 14, 16, 17, 32, 39, 42, 74, 76, 114-115, 118, 119, 165, 187, 188

Imperial War Museum 10, 33, 40, 43, 44, 45, 47, 50, 51, 52, 53, 54, 55, 56, 58, 59T, 60, 61, 62, 63, 64-65, 68, 69B, 72, 73, 82, 83, 84, 85, 88, 89L, 89R, 91B, 94, 95, 97L, 97R, 98, 101, 102L, 103, 104, 105L, 105R, 107, 108, 112, 113, 116, 117, 121, 135, 137, 153, 164, 184, 186

Kobal Collection 12, 36, 69T, 70, 99, 128, 129, 130

Maryhill Museum of Art /photo Laurent Sully Jaulmes 152L, 152R

Association Willy Maywald © ADAGP, Paris and DACS, London 1997 2, 154, 155, 174

Lee Miller Archives 41, 57, 67, 71, 75, 111, 124, 125, 132, 133, 134, 138, 140, 141, 142, 144, 146, 148, 149, 150

Musée de la Mode et du Costume, Paris /photo Christophe Walter 147

Popperfoto 9, 11, 22, 46, 48-49, 86-87, 90, 160, 162, 163, 166, 179, 182

Private Collections 59B, 78, 80, 109, 156, 157, 168, 169

Retrograph 34, 77, 123, 139

Printed by permission of the Norman Rockwell Family Trust © 1943 the Norman Rockwell Family Trust 66

Royal Academy of Arts, London 27

Sotheby's/Cecil Beaton Archive 23, 92, 184-185

Gallery Staley-Wise, New York, courtesy of the Estate of the late Louise Dahl-Wolfe 127, 131, 170, 171, 172

© Tate Gallery London 15

Topham Picture Source 79, 120, 161, 167